J 158 H238s

P9-DDB-741

DATE DUE

TO TEEN POWER

PAUL HARRINGTON

SIMON PULSE

NEW YORK LONDON TORONTO SYDNEY

NOTE TO READERS

This book contains the opinions and ideas of its author. It is intended to provide helpful and informative material on the subjects addressed in the publication; it is not intended to diagnose, prescribe, or treat any health disorder or other serious personal issue, nor is it guaranteeing any particular results. This book is sold with the understanding that the author and publisher are not engaged in rendering medical, health, or any other kind of personal professional services in the book, and the reader should consult with such person(s) before adopting any of the suggestions in this book or drawing inferences from it. The author and publisher specifically disclaim all responsibility for any liability, loss, or risk, personal or otherwise, which is incurred as a consequence, directly or indirectly, of the use and application of any of the contents of this book.

NSF-SFICOC-C0001801

The text paper in this book is acid-free and is sourced from forests managed in a sustainable manner. The Sustainable Forestry Initiative® program integrates the perpetual growing and harvesting of trees with the protection of wildlife, plants, soils, and water.

An imprint of Simon & Schuster Children's Publishing Division

1230 Avenue of the Americas,
New York, NY 10020

First Simon Pulse hardcover edition
September 2009

For information about special discounts for bulk purchases, please contact Simon & Schuster Special Sales at 1-866-506-1949 or business@simonandschuster.com.

Book design by Gozer Studio (Australia), www.gozer.com.au, directed by The Secret.

www.thesecret.tv

Manufactured in the United States of America

10 9 8 7 6 5 4 3 2 1

Library of Congress Control Number
2009932594

ISBN 978-1-4169-9498-5

ISBN 978-1-4169-9499-2 (eBook)

TS0159TTP_USBK09

"What this power is, I cannot say.
All I know is that it exists."
Alexander Graham Bell - inventor

CONTENTS

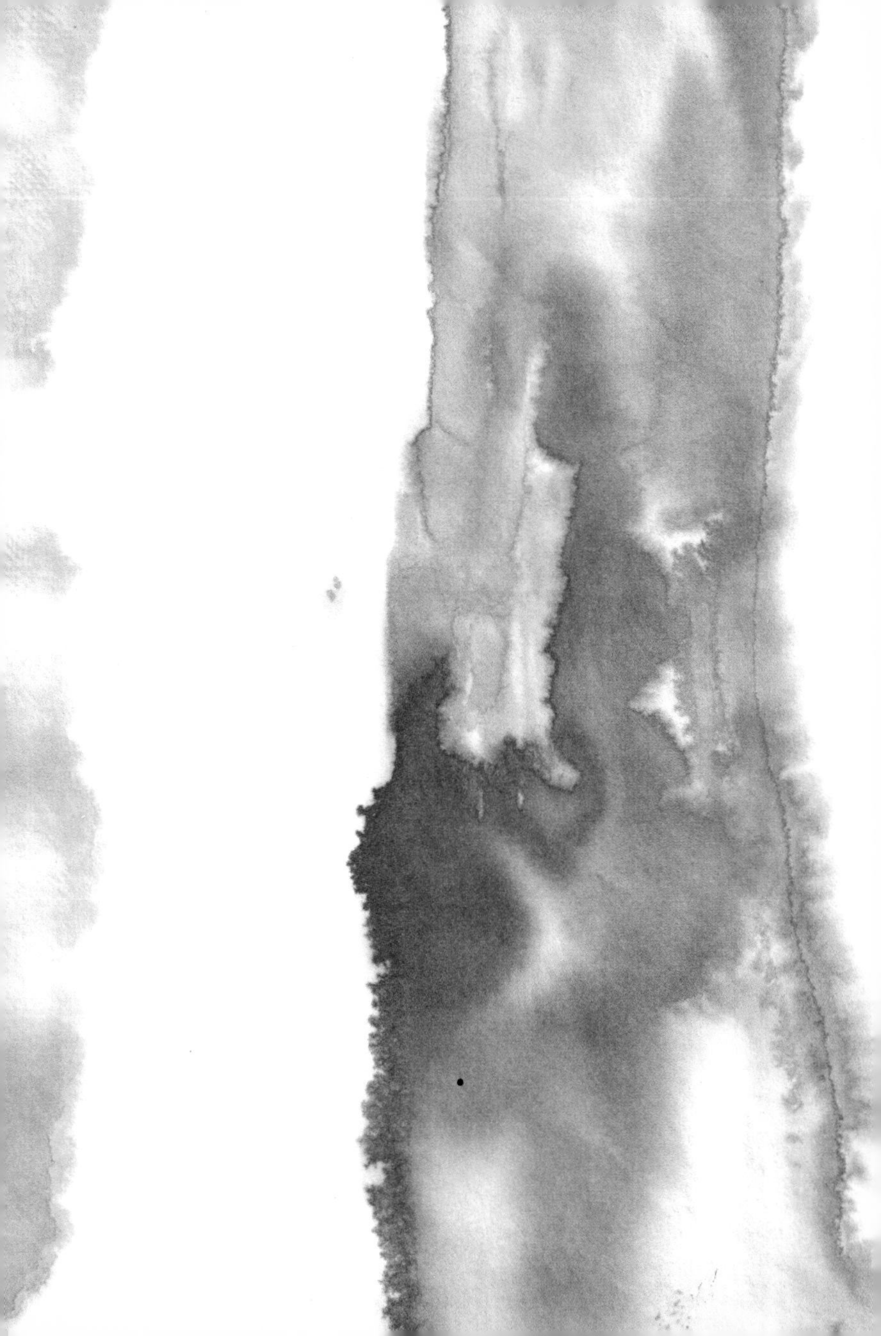

ACKNOWLEDGMENTS

This is the dullsville section where the author gets all gracious and thankful and maybe even a little self-indulgent...

Hello?

Are you still there?

Anyhow, since so many people totally deserve honest and heartfelt thanks for their contributions to this book, I'm going to push on regardless of whether or not anyone is still reading.

First of all, I want to thank Ross McNair, who was my co-conspirator, my creative sounding board, and my rock through the early stages of this project. Not only that, but you gave so many thoughts and ideas and insights and turns of phrase, particularly relating to money, health, relationships, and the world. You are a great teacher and a great friend, and I thank you.

To Colin Lee from Shift International for inspiring and cajoling me in the first place. In ***THE SECRET***, we highlight the importance of ASK, BELIEVE, and RECEIVE. Well, it was Colin who asked for this book. He truly believed in the need for a ***SECRET*** book for teens, and so I thank him for his enthusiastic encouragement.

To Jim Stynes, who gave so freely of his time and wisdom. Like Colin, Jim's organization, Reach, provides the most inspiring programs to help teenagers realize their potential and achieve their dreams. And there is no more inspiring leader and dreamer (and a gentleman to boot) than Big Jim.

To Jan Child, who has championed this project through to publication. Alongside her invaluable advice and brilliant creative contributions, Jan really stuck her neck out for me, and that is something I will always remember and cherish.

To the many story writers who contributed their own personal stories: this book is a lasting record of your courage, honesty, and willingness to give and to teach others all you have learned. I offer you all my most humble gratitude. Included among these: Rachael, Shiri, Michael, Michael, Elizabeth, Tien, Asher, Cassie, Jason, Shannon, Sam, Penelope, Yoshimitsu, KC, and Janice from Northwood University.

To Daniel Kerr, who clearly missed his calling as a private investigator. Your work in gathering and tracking down all the stories that appear throughout the book was simply marvelous.

To Skye Byrne for living ***THE SECRET*** every day, for your expert knowledge and advice, and for sensitively turning this book inside out as required.

To my outstanding creative design team, Cameron Boyle

and Nic George. Your bold cover artwork and sensitive and insightful page designs have taken this book to a whole different level. You guys rock.

To the team at Gozer Studio – Shamus Hoare, James Armstrong, and Luke Donovan – for the outstanding layout and graphic design, all done in record time. And might I add, Carn the Roos! Best football team in the entire world. (Hey, I did warn you that this would be self-indulgent!)

Many, many thanks to the team at Simon & Schuster: Darlene DeLillo, Dan Potash, Katherine Devendorf, Carolyn Reidy, Judith Curr, and most especially, Bethany Buck, whose velvet sledgehammer style of strong-willed yet sensitive book editing is so perfectly suited to bring out the best in this writer.

To my great friend Glenda Bell for coming aboard a year ago and quite literally keeping the wolves from the door. If it weren't for your tremendous support and dedication, I doubt I would have had the chance to finish this.

To Jessie Oldfield, Tim Patterson, and Damian Corboy, whose notes, suggestions, horrendous puns, and provocative conversations acted variously as my hand brake and my throttle, allowing me to keep it real. Cheers for that; it is so very much appreciated.

To Declan Keir-Saks, a teenage Aussie in LA, whose editorial notes ensured I stayed on track and didn't get too far ahead of myself. Thank you.

To the Chicago suits, Bob Rainone and Don Zyck, in fact

not just suits but more like our very own Secret Blues Brothers, whose one-track mission from God appears to be to take our wild ideas and deliver them to the world.

To Mike Gardiner and all his compadres taking care of ***THE SECRET***... I'm happy to say that you ***can*** handle the truth! Thank you for keeping the dream alive.

To ***THE SECRET*** team members: Andrea Keir, Josh Gold, Raph Kilpatrick, Hayley Byrne, Laura Jensen, and Chye Lee; the Chicago crew: Danielle Likvan, Sibel Rainone, Andi Roeder, Lori Sharapov, Susan Seah, Kyle Koch, and Mindy Hankinson; and the website warriors: Mark O'Connor, John Herren, and Jimmy Palmer... thank you all for your tireless support, suggestions, and encouragement.

To my family, Megan and Paige, thank you so much for believing in me and telling me that I'm cool, even when I'm wearing a purple velvet suit. And to Asher, my teenage inspiration and the specific reason this book was written. I dedicate this to you and thank you for your comments and advice, and especially for not telling me that I'm totally lame. Well, not every day, at least. I hope more than anything that through this book, you come to believe in your dreams.

And, of course, to Rhonda Byrne, my boss, my mentor, and my best friend... thank you, thank you, thank you for trusting in me, for believing in me, and for inviting me on this wondrous journey. Your boundless generosity and spirit continue to inspire me and light up the path. It goes without saying that there could be no *Secret to Teen Power* without ***THE SECRET*** in the first place, and I especially thank you for sharing that ***SECRET***, not just with me, but with the entire world. You once gave me a book, and it changed my life. I now offer you this book in return. It's not Wallace Wattles, but it comes with all of my heart.

Finally, to the casual reader who has taken the time to read this mushy stuff without falling asleep... I bet you hang in there through the end credits of every movie, too. Good for you... a bit weird, but hey, it's your call; you paid your money, so knock yourself out. If you happen to be a teenager or thereabouts, then please read on, open your heart and mind to a whole new way of thinking and feeling and being, then step off and watch all your dreams come true. I double dare you.

This book is for ***YOU***.

Love and blessings,

PAUL HARRINGTON

INTRODUCTION

STRAIGHT UP

So what's the deal with this so-called ***SECRET*** that everyone's been talking about? The word is, it lets you have, do, or be anything you choose. Sound good? Maybe a little too good?

The truth is, ***THE SECRET*** helps bring riches to the poor, abundance to the hungry, peace to the war-torn, wellness to the unhealthy. But it can also help make dreams come true...for you. Maybe you don't think you deserve it. But you do. And if you can dream it, you have the power to make it happen. Seriously.

Now, it might seem obvious, but the hardest part about living your dream is knowing just exactly ***what your dream is.***

Remember when you were a little kid, and you had no limits? Adults would say, "What do you want to be when you grow up?" And you'd say, "An astronaut," "A doctor," "A ballet dancer," or "A football player." You could be anything you wanted.

And then you got older, and there were all these pressures and expectations and demands and limitations. You got bombarded with reasons why you wouldn't be able to live out those dreams. People started telling you you're not smart enough, not strong enough, not pretty enough, not *good* enough. It's like your life's ambitions somehow got hijacked by the grown-up world.

So...what if there was a ***SECRET*** that would let you live your dreams? What if you could get back to that time in your life when there were no limits to what you could be? And what if you discovered you have the power to make all your dreams come true – to go anywhere, to do anything, to be everything you choose?

Would you listen?

Well...do you want to know a ***SECRET***?

THE SECRET REVEALED

WHAT'S THE BIG SECRET?

Okay, so you've been kept in the dark for way too long. It's time to learn the truth – the actual factuals, so to speak. And the truth is, this big ***SECRET*** you've been hearing about... well, it really does unleash the power to let you be all you can be and achieve all you want to achieve.

Miracles of health, wealth, success, relationships, happiness, freedom, love... all these things are available to you once you know ***THE SECRET***.

So what exactly *is* ***THE SECRET***?

According to science, there are certain laws that govern the Universe. There's the law of gravity – whatever goes up must come down. And there's Einstein's law of relativity – everything in the Universe is made of energy. And then there's "string theory" – everything in the Universe vibrates, everything has its own vibe.

But the most powerful law in the entire Universe is... ***the law of attraction.***

THE SECRET is the ***law of attraction.***

Everything that happens in your life all comes down to attraction. You attract all the stuff that happens to you, every last little thing, no matter whether it's totally awesome or truly awful. It's all about you.

And you do it with the power of your thoughts. Whatever you think about, that's what goes down, that's what happens.

A UNIVERSAL POWER SOURCE

See, your thoughts are like this Universal power source, a force of nature - what you think about, you bring about. You are creating your life according to what's going on in your mind right at this moment. Now, that might sound like Jedi mind tricks, but it's totally real. All the major religions all over the world are on board with this, including Hinduism, Judaism, Christianity, Buddhism, and Islam. And many civilizations and cultures over the past five thousand years have also tapped into the power of thought through this great Universal law.

But enough of the history lesson. For now, you just need to know this one thing: the law of attraction says ***like attracts like***. That's the bottom line, the heart and soul of this Universal law.

It's just like that saying, "Birds of a feather flock together." In other words, a flock of birds is just like a group of friends; they're drawn together because of all the stuff they have in common. They're tight because they're alike and they like all the same things - like attracts like. That's the law of attraction in action.

But of course it's not necessarily about looking exactly alike or being exactly the same. Your friends are not all clones. You don't look alike, but you almost certainly *think* alike, and you like one another because of this. Like attracts like - that's the law of attraction.

And according to the law of attraction, it's your thoughts that hold the power, that do all the attracting. For example, have you ever had a thought about a song? Then, before you know it, you're thinking about that song all day long until the song is totally stuck in your head. And eventually you'll be hearing that song being played everywhere you go because now you're fully obsessing. Now you're attracting the song - in the mall, at school, on TV - wherever you are, your thoughts are attracting that song.

THOUGHTS BECOME THINGS

The law of attraction means your thoughts become things.

Amazing, huh? It's like, the life you're living is all due to the thoughts you're thinking.

"If you're going to be thinking anyway, you may as well think big."

Donald Trump - *real estate entrepreneur*

Successful people seem to know this stuff instinctively, while those who struggle don't. That's why they attract failure. Either way, you create your own reality, your good fortune and your *mis*fortune. It all just comes down to your thinking.

Okay, let's crank it up a level. The law of attraction is really responsible for *everything*. All the stuff that goes on in your life is all down to your thoughts. And whether you realize it or not, you're always thinking. Watching TV, when you're online, playing video games, or watching the clock in school, you never stop thinking. And it's these thoughts that are creating your future life. Your current life is a perfect reflection of thoughts you've had in the past. It's like payback from way back. What you think about *right now* will inevitably be attracted back to you as your life to come.

"All that we are is the result of what we have thought.... What we think, we become."
Buddha – spiritual teacher

THE GOOD, THE BAD, AND THE UGLY

Whenever anything happens – whether it's good or bad, happy or sad – it's all the law of attraction. ***YOU'RE*** the one attracting it. For example, you find five dollars on the sidewalk. ***YOU*** attracted it. Someone you lost touch with friends you on Facebook. ***YOU*** attracted that. Or maybe you chance upon some amazing clothes on sale; the right size, last ones on the rack. ***YOU*** attracted all of it.

And on the flip side, stuff that isn't so hot - like a pop quiz when you haven't done your homework, or a pimple when you're due to meet your crush - ***YOU*** attracted that too.

Okay, so you're thinking, *"How could I create a pimple? How am I attracting that?"*

All right, here's the deal.... Remember, Einstein figured out that everything in the Universe is made of energy. So everything you can see, all that you touch or taste or hold, is all made up of the exact same stuff - energy. Beyond the molecules and atoms and electrons and whatnot, at a sub-microscopic level, everything is simply energy. And guess what? That includes ***YOU***.

But here's another head spin: your *thoughts* are also energy.

Check it out: doctors use machines like EEGs and brain scans to measure the energy released by your brain activity. It turns out, your brain is transmitting energy with every thought. So your thoughts really *are* energy.

"The energy of the mind is the essence of life."
Aristotle – philosopher

And when this thought energy, or *vibe* that you transmit, is in perfect sync with the stuff you're thinking about, you create a powerful magnetic attraction - like attracts like. It's totally mind-blowing stuff, that everything you think about is attracted to you.

TOTAL CONTROL

Another way to look at it is that you're like this ultimate Universal remote control. Normally, a remote control can tune in to the TV, DVD player, MP3 player, game console, and surround sound system. With one click, an infrared signal changes the channel, turns up the sound, plays music, or launches a game or a movie. It does whatever you want, simply by sending out a different signal.

Well, you're even more powerful than that because you can control your entire experience. Just like the remote control, all you have to do is send out a different signal.

Say, for example, you've had a falling out with your friends and no one is talking to you. Your thoughts are consumed with bitterness, resentment, and loneliness. And that's what you experience. In order to change the channel, to change what you experience, you need to send out a new signal. You need to have thoughts of contentment, happiness, and friendliness. And then your friends will all come around.

And that's the way you can change everything, all the experiences of your life as well as the world around you. It really is just like changing the channel. But instead of with an infrared signal, you do it with the power of your thoughts.

WHAT YOU THINK ABOUT, YOU BRING ABOUT

The fact is, you attract into your life the stuff that you think about most, and you also *become* whatever you think about most. And that makes it critically important to think about stuff you want the most!

> *"A man is but the product of his thoughts.*
> *What he thinks, he becomes."*
> Mahatma Gandhi – spiritual leader

Problem is, if you're like most people, you spend way too much time thinking about what's wrong in your life, or stuff you don't want. And guess what? Bad stuff happens. You fight with your parents. Or your text won't send. Then you complain about this stuff happening, and guess what? *More* bad stuff happens.

DOS AND DON'TS

No matter what you think about, it's going to happen. That's the law. So if you make an effort to think about all the good things in life – things you like, things you want to happen – then that's what you'll attract; that's what happens. Because you know what they say, "Stuff happens." You just have to make sure it's good stuff.

Some people, even when they know ***THE SECRET***, still make the classic mistake of thinking about stuff they ***don't*** want. Like:

- I ***don't*** want to be rejected.
- I ***don't*** want a bad grade.
- I ***don't*** want to gain weight.

But you see, in each case, they're thinking about what they don't want. If you do that, you'll stress out, you'll give off a stressed-out vibe, and then you'll attract exactly what you don't want. It's like you may as well be saying:

- I ***want*** to be publicly dumped and humiliated.
- I ***want*** my D– posted for the whole school to see.
- I ***want*** to split the seams on my favorite jeans.

You just can't think like that and expect that it won't happen. You have to change it up to reflect and project exactly what you ***do*** want. For instance:

- I am popular and have lots of awesome friends.
- I always ace my exams.
- I look great in all my clothes.

And that's what you'll attract; that's what you'll be.

NO IFS OR BUTS

The law of attraction always gives you exactly what you *think* about, but without the qualifications, the "ifs," "buts," and "don't wants."

Now, that might sound like the Universe has selective hearing, like when your dad asks your brother or sister to take out the recycling, and they swear he never did.

But in fact it's more like a focus on keywords. Just like a search engine - Google, Yahoo, iTunes, whatever.

Let's say you're browsing for music online. But you're not a fan of punk, emo, or pop, so you type in something like "*NO* Fall Out Boy, My Chemical Romance, or Katy Perry."

What you'll find is that the search engine completely ignores the "*no*" and focuses only on the keywords. It'll give you hundreds of fanboy sites for these artists - exactly what you *didn't* want. You scored the keyword and nothing more.

And it's the same with the law of attraction. You always attract the keywords, the key subject of your thoughts. You think and obsess about something you don't want to happen, but it happens anyway. So why is that? It's because you focused on the very thing you didn't want, the subject, so the Universe conspired to give you that very thing. The only way to get what you really want in life is to focus precisely on what you ***do*** want.

HEROES

Shane Gould

A fifteen-year-old girl by the name of Shane Gould arrived at the Olympics having smashed the world record in swimming over every distance from 100 meters up to 1500 meters. She was a total phenomenon, the likes of which the world had never seen.

Upon reaching the Olympic finals, Gould was confronted by her major rivals, who arrived on the pool deck wearing T-shirts with the words "Everything that glitters is not necessarily ***Gould****." Think about that: genuine, world-class gold medal contenders indulging in psychological taunts! And the result of their trash talk? Gould became the first female swimmer to win three individual gold medals at an Olympics, with all of the wins in world-record time.*

What we learn from the Shane Gould story – at least from the perspective of her competitors – is that you just can't focus on what you don't want (in their case, Gould's winning gold), because that's what you'll get. So don't sweat someone else winning gold. . . . Go for yours.

MY SO-CALLED LIFE

Sometimes we let life get us down. We get into a funk when things don't go our way, and then it all spirals downward from there. Negative thoughts attract a negative situation. And more negative thoughts attract even worse conditions, and before you know it, you find yourself bitter and angry and surrounded by misery.

Have you ever noticed that negative, angry people who find lots to complain about, and who seem to whine most of the time, end up miserable *all* the time? They have a bad vibe. And they're usually surrounded by other negative, angry people. That's what they attract. That's their life.

"Negative people can sap your energy so fast, and they can take your dreams from you too."
Magic Johnson – basketball champion

And then there are the chilled-out, friendly people who are always looking on the bright side. They lead happy lives, and they're usually surrounded by other chilled-out, happy people. It's all a function of thought – your life is really just a reflection of your vibe and the thoughts you hold on to.

So what sort of life do you want? What are your major thoughts? What's your vibe?

NO FLAW IN THE LAW

We all attract with every thought we have, and the law of attraction responds without fail. If it seems like the law failed you because you don't have what you want, well, the truth is the law didn't fail, it already responded to you. If you don't have what you want, your thoughts must have been focused on the *absence* of what you want. You noticed it wasn't there and that set up another attraction . . . the attraction of *not* getting what you want.

It's like when you're on a sports team . . . baseball, soccer, lacrosse, whatever. Come the first game, when the team sheet gets posted on the notice board, you see your name's not in the starting lineup. So you get mad at the coach. You begin to develop an attitude. Each week, you check the team sheet. And each week, just as you suspected, your name is missing. Why is that? It's because you are reacting to the absence of what you want. You're reacting to the disappointment of not being able to start. You're sending out a powerful vibe: "I'm not on the team." And the Universe responds, through your coach and teammates, keeping you "not on the team." Keep that up and eventually you'll get cut from the team entirely. And you sure don't want that. Instead, you have to think, "I ***AM*** on the team," whether you're starting the game or warming the bench. Because in all circumstances, with everything, you have to focus on what you really want, not on what you don't want.

WE ARE MAGNETS

Some more science. We live in an electromagnetic Universe, and everything attracts. That means you, me, everybody, and everything in the Universe is magnetic.

What's more, as magnets we attract all those things that we are most like. Everything that comes into our lives, we've attracted magnetically.

And given that thoughts are also energy, with their own vibe and their own magnetic properties, that means your thoughts attract things, your thoughts become things, and therefore, your mind shapes the world around you. Our thoughts are drawing things into our lives, just like a magnet.

Don't stress out if you're not getting all this technical stuff. It's not like you need to know how to fire up a nuclear fission reactor to turn on the light switch. You just need to have a little faith that it works, and that you can use it to have, do, or be whatever you choose.

REAL STORIES

Rachael's Secret

When I was in third grade, I told my mother that I wanted to go to the University of Notre Dame. I remember going to meetings at age thirteen about what it took to get in – that's how bad I wanted it. Notre Dame will not accept someone merely because they got a good score on the SAT. It takes so much more. I knew everything it took and used this knowledge to my advantage.

I told everyone I talked to, new friends and old friends, that I would be attending the University of Notre Dame. The response was almost ALWAYS the same: "Wow, isn't that school hard to get into? Don't you have to be really smart?" They would wish me good luck in a "you really need it" tone. I never let this sway me.

Before every football game, Notre Dame would play a commercial showing a girl taking "the letter" out of her mailbox. I CRIED EVERY TIME (because I could FEEL – with so much intensity – how I would feel when I came to that day).

When it came time to apply, I was more stressed out than I had ever been in my life, but I still continued to tell people that I would be going there. Sometimes a thought would creep into my head, saying, "What if I've been telling everyone that I'm going there and then I don't get in?" Every time I'd stop and say, "NO, I will not let myself think these thoughts." And I would continue to imagine and to feel the feelings of coming home and seeing the letter sitting on the table.

On March 28, 2008, I got a call from my stepfather telling me that I had to come home "RIGHT NOW." When I got home, I saw the envelope and felt every feeling that I had felt previously in my mind – only magnified.

The letter said "Welcome Home."

I have never wanted anything more in my entire life. I have never KNOWN something more intensely. I KNEW that Notre Dame was the place for me, was my home (I guess God, the Universe, knew too).

Rachael, age 18
Indiana, USA

CARPE DIEM - SEIZE THE DAY

So many people live for tomorrow instead of today. It's as if life begins when you get your driver's license, or when you graduate, or when you move away from your parents. It's all *when, when, when.* But that's not living today.

A huge part of the ***SECRET*** is that all of your power is concentrated today, in the moment, this very instant, *right now*. What you think about the most or focus on the most right now will turn up as your life in the future. It's like payback from *not* so way back. That is to say, you can't be angry and frustrated today and expect things to improve tomorrow. Focus on today, get satisfaction *now*, because that's the only way your dreams of tomorrow come true.

"We are the music-makers,
And we are the dreamers of dreams"
Arthur O'Shaughnessy - poet
as quoted in Willy Wonka & the Chocolate Factory

You might be thinking to yourself, "Hang on a sec, I'm not ready to live my dream. I haven't even *figured out* my dream."

Well, let's deal with that right now.

THE SECRET 101

What do *you* want to do? Who do *you* want to be?

Don't know? Relax, those are pretty deep questions. But you know, the answer is probably sitting there right under your nose. All you have to do is be conscious of the things that really get you excited. Seriously. It's more likely than not that what you want to do, and who you're supposed to be, are all tied up with the stuff that fires you up right now. So...

Take out a notepad and write a list of all the stuff that you're into, awesome stuff that takes your breath away and really makes you feel all warm and fuzzy.

No pressure; just write down anything that you love to do, or that you really look forward to. It could be school related, or things you do with friends. Maybe it's stuff you do on your own. Or something you've always wanted to do. Whatever you can think of, just write it down.

Go ahead, do it right now.

......

You didn't do it, did you? I bet you figured, "Eh, I'll do it some other time." Well this *is* the time. This is your moment. This is your big opportunity to take a chance, to shine.

"A lot of people are afraid to say what they want. That's why they don't get what they want."
Madonna – *singer, actor*

Truth is, most people just go with the flow; they stick with the flock. Well, that's up to you. The choice is yours, to be a follower and get what's given. Or you can step up and take what's yours.

You're into that? Okay, great, so write down a list of all the things that thrill you, that make you feel great. Go ahead. What have you got to lose?

To get your creative juices flowing, here are some random suggestions:

- Acting
- Animals
- Art
- Blogging
- Business
- Cars
- Computers
- Dancing
- The environment
- Fashion
- Gaming
- Health
- History
- Journalism

- Motorbikes
- Movies
- Music
- Politics
- Science
- Singing
- Skateboarding
- Sports
- Surfing
- Technology
- Volunteering
- Writing

If your passion isn't here, no worries. Just be true to yourself and make out your list. To make it easier, picture yourself doing each one of the things you're interested in. Imagine with all your senses - the sights, the sounds, the smells, the sensations - feel the buzz, feel the excitement. Which moments feel best?

Now cut the list down to your three absolute favorites. Be decisive; be strong.

Okay, done?

Go you! Because these three things are your purpose, your passion, and your motivation in life.

And *this* is what life is all about. This is your ***SECRET*** power, ***THE SECRET*** revealed!

THE SECRET MADE SIMPLE

BREAKIN' DOWN THE BIG S

So now you've heard the word on the law of attraction. And for some of you, all this talk of laws may well have you thinking, "Well, not all laws apply to me."

But the law of attraction applies to everyone and everything. You can't break this law and you can't avoid it. However, when you harness the law of attraction, you can do whatever you want to do and be whatever you want to be, regardless of your religion, race, ethnicity, age, sex, or finances.

That's because the law of attraction is a Universal law; just like the law of gravity, it applies equally to all people no matter who you are or where you spring from. And that means there's no secret handshake that lets you off the hook even if you happen to be rich or famous.

Consider Tony Hawk. Even though he's king of the half-pipe, he still gets his share of bone-crushing injuries. That's because gravity doesn't play favorites; certainly not toward famous skaters with lucrative endorsement deals, or anyone else, for that matter. Gravity is a Universal law, and it applies equally to all people. Likewise the law of attraction.

IT'S NOT FAIR

The other thing that occurs to people is, what's with all the bad stuff that goes down, the stuff you see on the news? Where's the law of attraction in all that?

Well, the sad reality is, victims of tragedy didn't ask for their fate (and they totally didn't deserve it). They probably didn't even know they were capable of attracting stuff. But still, there's an attraction. And that's because the law of attraction operates whether you know about it or not. Most of the world is running on autopilot.

Think of it like this: you listen to music on an MP3 player - iPod, cell phone, whatever. You select a favorite playlist or you choose track-by-track exactly what you want to hear. That's like attracting just what you want, when you want it. On the other hand, you can go with the random shuffle mode; the device gives you random songs in a random order, whether you like the songs or not. You get what you're given, and you don't get to choose.

Many of the sad stories and tragedies you see on the evening news are just like that. People who don't know ***THE SECRET*** are attracting by default. They're on shuffle and they attract stuff they don't want without even meaning to. They've been conditioned to believe that you get what you're given in life, whether that's a random, unwanted song or a tornado on your doorstep.

So how can you avoid these tragedies? The solution is simple: don't live life on shuffle. Do your own attracting by thinking for yourself. Create your own thoughts of hope and optimism, and let those thoughts take flight so you take control of your own future.

> *You have a choice right now. Do you want to believe that it's just the luck of the draw and bad things can happen to you at any time? Do you want to believe that you can be in the wrong place at the wrong time? That you have no control over circumstances?*
>
> *Or do you want to believe and* ***know*** *that your life experience is in your hands and that only all* ***good*** *can come into your life because that is the way you think? You have a choice, and whatever you choose to think* ***will*** *become your life experience....*
>
> *Your life is in your hands. No matter where you are now, no matter what has happened in your life, you can begin to consciously choose your thoughts, and you can change your life.*

Rhonda Byrne

THE SECRET

"Luck is when an opportunity comes along and you're prepared for it."
Denzel Washington – actor

WHAT WAS I THINKING?

Another thing people stress out about once they come to grips with ***THE SECRET*** is the fear that they have to stay focused on all their thoughts *all* the time. *Good* thoughts... *Bad* thoughts... *Do* want... *Don't* want... It's a nightmare!

Now get this: you have at least sixty thousand thoughts a day. And with that many thoughts bouncing around in your head, it may seem very hard to control them. What you *can* do is focus on how you're feeling.

See, when you're feeling good, you can't help but think good thoughts. And those good thoughts attract more good thoughts and even more good feelings. And that sets up the attraction for all the great stuff to come your way. That's when you know you're on a roll, a lucky streak, a perfect day.

But if you're feeling stressed or depressed, that tells you that your thoughts are hedging on the dark side. And that often leads to a spiral of bad thoughts and bad feelings. Things go from bad to worse, and it's a vicious cycle, a very bad day.

Like when something goes wrong in the morning – there's no hot water for your shower, or the milk for your cereal has gone sour. And everything just spirals downward from there, one unlucky break after another.

What you maybe don't realize is that it all started with one negative thought, which attracted more bad thoughts and bad feelings until something bad happened, which then attracted a bad reaction and more bad thoughts and bad feelings, and suddenly your whole vibe is locked into this chain reaction of bad attractions. You're stuck in a losing streak.

So if you ever find yourself having one of those days, you have to realize that it isn't caused by the bad stuff happening around you. That's just the effect. It's caused by your feelings and what you're thinking. And once you know that, you'll be able to turn a bad day around just by changing the way you're thinking and feeling.

The idea is to stay aware, and to ask yourself, "How am I feeling now? How is my vibe?" If you're buzzing with excitement, you'll be attracting awesome stuff. But if you're feeling anger, resentment, depression, or fear, your thoughts are totally bleak...and so is what you're attracting.

HEROES

Daniel Johns

The three members of grunge band Silverchair burst onto the scene when they were barely teens. Acclaimed worldwide, their early success came at a cost. Lead singer and songwriter Daniel Johns was stressed out of his mind, with all the music industry pressure and the touring, recording, publicity, demands on time, and expectations of further success. And worse, Johns was assaulted by hater thugs who recognized him in the street. He became reclusive, suffered anxiety, and developed an eating disorder.

Understandably, Johns came to resent music, yet he kept performing against his will. In fact, the teen angst he was singing about was not just an act; he was practically drowning in it. And that's when he reached the decision that he really didn't want to feel that way anymore. And, more important, he didn't want to create music while feeling that way. So he did something totally unexpected. He took the master tapes of the just completed Silverchair album Diorama, and erased them. Every track! As he explained to his bandmates, it's crucial that you feel good when you're creating, or else what are you creating? What are you attracting?

Daniel Johns turned his thoughts, his emotions, and his whole vibe around, and together with Silverchair he re-recorded the entire album. And that Diorama album

> *became the critical breakthrough record of their career, all thanks to Daniel Johns making a decision to change his thoughts and, more important, change his feelings.*

Your thoughts create the attraction. Your thoughts are the power, the energy, the magnet. Your thoughts are the primary cause of all the stuff that happens. But it's your feelings that tell you whether your thoughts are attracting the good life or blocking you from it.

If your feelings are telling you that your thoughts are attracting bad stuff, then obviously it's time to change your thoughts, pronto. Bad feelings and a plummeting vibe are like an early warning system. They're like this great big wailing siren going off above your head.

SWITCH IT UP

So when your plummeting vibe is telling you that your own thoughts are blocking the good life and attracting bad stuff, you know you have to switch things up. But how? The answer is simple: whatever it takes. Just find a way to change the way you feel. Break the cycle. Do something different.

Maybe you could go blading or riding or jogging...any sort of exercise. Or just breathe in the fresh air - feel the sunshine, the wind in your hair, or the rain on your skin. Listen to the sounds; soak up the colors. Close your eyes and just feel alive.

Or maybe try music. That's another great option to change your mood. Of course, you have to take care that the tracks you're tuning in to match the vibe you're aiming for. Let's say you're feeling stressed or depressed about something. Like maybe you just got dumped, or blown off by your latest crush. So what do you do? Go home and play some depressing breakup songs? Some really heavy emo tunes? No way! That's like gorging on a box of Krispy Kremes because you feel fat. Seriously, it's not helping.

Instead, you have to suck it up and do the opposite. Play some feel-good tracks. Crank up SingStar or Guitar Hero. Whatever it takes. Because if you want to shift your mood to feel better and have better thoughts, you just can't wallow in self-pity.

Try it out. Put on a tune. Preferably something upbeat, something that makes you feel great. And sing. Seriously, do the whole karaoke thing. Just like those randoms you see with their iPods on, belting out a tune like an off-key *Idol* wannabe. They don't care; the singing is making them happy. And that's because their *vibe* is totally in tune with the song.

It's the same deal with dancing. That's why a lot of house and techno music is so great to dance to. You pick up on the rhythm and your whole body syncs to the beat in this great harmony of heart-thumping, lung-busting, foot-stomping, feel-fantastic energy... it's intense. All that stuff is sure to change your mood, lift your vibe, and make you feel alive.

BORN TO BE ALIVE

And that right there is another secret behind ***THE SECRET***. Simply: feel alive, feel fantastic, feel ecstatic! It's the fastest way to attract the life of your dreams. Focus on radiating out into the Universe those feelings of joy and happiness. And as you radiate feelings of joy and happiness, they'll be reflected back to you as the experiences of your future life.

Now, that might all sound easier said than done. Like, you're in a total funk and you're expected to flip the switch and just "get happy"? I mean, it's not like you can just select your feelings off the rack. Or click on a smiley emoticon.

Wouldn't it be great if in real life you could just select a drop-down menu, double-click the happy face anytime you like and choose the way you feel? Well, even though some people do that, most of us can't. But don't worry, there is another way you can go about making yourself happy whenever you choose. And that's by taking baby steps and graduating up the scale of feelings.

SCALE YOUR FEELINGS

Let's say you're in despair and depression. Like when your boyfriend or girlfriend has dumped you. That's major depression - it's about as low as you can go, the lowest vibe. But instead of just trying to get happy, which is a much higher vibe, you need to shift your feelings to something that's closer to where you're at. Rather than bottling yourself up in despair (and then worrying about what else you'll attract!), shift your feelings up bit by bit to frustration and annoyance. "Who is he (or she) to break up with *me?*"

The next feeling you're aiming for is boredom, which you can reach by thinking disinterested thoughts like "Whatever... my ex didn't deserve me anyway."

After that comes mild satisfaction; think of something that makes you feel kind of okay. "There are plenty more fish in the sea."

Keep going the same way until you feel hope, then enthusiasm, then happiness, passion, joy, and finally, love.

And in love, your vibe is really buzzing; it's the highest possible frequency. In love, you'll attract so many things to inspire you. And whether that's love for another person, or for a place or experiences or things you love to do, that feeling of love is the perfect antidote for despair and depression. And simply by taking these incremental baby steps to feel good, you'll find that achieving love, or anything else you want, is not so hard after all.

REAL STORIES

Shiri's Secret

At the start of my last year at school, twelfth grade, I was pretty much depressed. In all my eleven years of school I was never sure of myself, never had real friends, never had a bit of fun, and if I did it was rare. I was behind when it came to studying, I lived an unhealthy lifestyle, I used to stay out three times a week, and I had bad relationships with my family. I knew my life was heading in a bad direction, and all I wanted was to change it. I had no idea how, and no plan. I just wanted badly to change it.

So I started to study and stopped hanging out with the people who influenced me badly. I tried to change my lifestyle, but it just did not work. I realized I was not going forward (even though I was willing it) because I still thought in the wrong way, and I should change that.

So I forced myself to feel good. Since then, my life turned out to be GOLD. It happened like magic! I received even more than I asked for!

At first it was with studying. I forced myself to believe I DO know, I AM smart, and then my grades started to go higher and higher till I had top grades from all nine classes at school. I didn't study too much, either! One to two days studying was enough for me, while other students were studying for a week plus.

After that, I forced myself to feel I'm loved. I asked for true friends. I don't know how, but I suddenly found great friends and soul mates in my school, when I was SURE I couldn't relate to anyone. People love me, even the ones who used to hate me. One time a girl who was known for hating me lost her car keys at school, and I found them. She and her friends thanked me and said, "The whole school is talking so good about you now." I was happy, because I had been pretty much hated in my school. That was A HUGE change for me.

Every possible thing I had problems with in my life turned out to be good, because I forced myself to feel good, I forced myself to feel loved, I forced myself to feel wanted, and in the end I got it.

My advice: BELIEVE, BELIEVE, BELIEVE! It will PAY off for the BEST!

Shiri, age 18
Kiryat Shmona, Israel

IT'S YOUR CALL

It's in your hands; you can choose to feel good now, or you can put it off for another day, week, month, or maybe longer. In fact, you can stay miserable as long as it suits you. But here's a little secret: misery doesn't suit you, it's not your style, and you don't wear it well.

So then, what do you choose? To feel good now?

Because this is the bottom line: feeling good is totally your birthright. And feeling good now is what it's all about. Feeling good now changes all of your tomorrows.

Feeling good is ***THE SECRET***.

And the greatest secret is just feel good!

THE SECRET 101

A lot of people get into computer role-playing games like World of Warcraft or Grand Theft Auto. There's that whole immersion in the virtual world, the adventure and the thrills of life-and-death situations. But the best part is, you can just press pause when things turn sour.

Wouldn't it be good if you could do that in real life? Especially when things aren't going so well, when you're stressed, or when you just don't feel good.

Well, as a matter of fact, just like in role-playing games, you *can* press pause to take a time-out on life, so you can then focus on shifting your feelings.

And in order to shift your feelings, it's cool to have up your sleeve a ***SECRET SHIFTER*** or two. That's a *mood* shifter, something that makes you feel instantly happy. Something you can recall at any time to make you feel great and re-energize you so you're ready to re-enter the game of life.

Maybe it's an awesome memory, a flashback of a funny moment. Or good times with your best friends, a great vacation, or a classic song, or maybe even a picture of your latest crush. What are your greatest and most precious memories? Maybe it's a combination of all these things, like a montage of memories.

So think about your montage. Write down a list of things that bring a smile to your face every time you think of them. And anytime you're feeling stressed or depressed or angry or unhappy, look at your list, recall your montage, and just *FEEL GOOD*. And that's the key to the good life. The power of ***THE SECRET***...made simple.

HOW TO USE THE SECRET

A GUIDE FOR NEWBS

For some people, the idea of being a "Creator" can seem pretty intense. Like that's a job title reserved for Leonardo da Vinci. Or William Shakespeare. Or Jane Austen. But the truth is, you *are* a Creator, and you're creating your life through the law of attraction.

And it's no coincidence that just like you, many creative artists and master storytellers have tapped ***THE SECRET*** in paintings and plays and poetry and prose since the dawn of civilization.

Think of all the fairy tales, fables, myths, and legends from your childhood. The law of attraction is always there. Check it out: the hero has a dream, something he desires right from the bottom of his heart. And when he dreams long enough and wishes hard enough and proves himself worthy enough, a mystical force makes the dream come true.

ONCE UPON A TIME...

In classic fairy tales, the law of attraction is the wishing star, the magic beans, or the fairy godmother. In movies, it's the Force, or the One Ring that rules them all. Or the Genie who emerges from the lamp to grant Aladdin's every wish.

You see, the Genie, the Force, the One Ring, and ***THE SECRET***... they're all the same deal. It's like you have your very own Genie, your own Force, your own fairy godmother or magic beans or wishing star, only it's called the law of attraction. But unlike these fantasy stories, the law of attraction is the *real* deal; it's a Universal force, and it's there to serve you. It doesn't judge you or test you or make you prove your worthiness; it simply listens to your every thought, your every wish, your every desire. And it makes all your dreams come true.

HEROES

Walt Disney

If you were looking for the biggest dreamer in the history of Hollywood or maybe even the world, you could make a pretty good case that it's Walt Disney. The man who created the mouse, not to mention the Magic Kingdom and a library of classic fairy-tale movies, also lived his life as a daydreamer who refused to face reality. Disney was renowned for hanging tough with his vision regardless of the opposition he was facing – bankruptcy, having his ideas stolen, or facing criticism and derision by all the so-called experts of Hollywood and Wall Street. Disney proved them all wrong.

At just twenty-one years of age, he and his brother Roy scraped together sufficient funds to build a studio and a team of hotshot animators. He then created a successful series called Oswald the Lucky Rabbit. But his distribu-

tor poached the entire staff, and worse, duped him out of the Oswald character. But Disney didn't let that destroy him. He just got on with dreaming big, believing in miracles, and allowing magic to happen. And that's when he created a certain talking mouse.

And the rest, as they say, is history. And what a history... Disney was the first to use synchronized sound in cartoons, the first to use color, the first to make an animated feature, and the first to build a theme park. Disney was undoubtedly one of the great dreamers, and all of his dreams came true.

"If you can dream it, you can do it. Always remember that this whole thing was started with a dream and a mouse."
Walt Disney – movie maker, entrepreneur

If you've got big dreams like Disney, or even modest aspirations, you'll be happy to learn about this two-thousand-year-old Creative Process that helps you tap your very own inner Genie. But unlike Disney's Genie, this Creative Process doesn't limit you to just three wishes. In fact, you can have as many as you choose.

THE CREATIVE PROCESS

You may have heard the phrase, "Ask and you shall receive." Now, whether you happen to be Christian, Muslim, Hindu, or Jewish, or whether you dance to the beat of a whole different drum, the lesson remains the same: all that you desire, all that you seek, all that you ask for can be achieved through a simple three-step Creative Process.

ASK...BELIEVE...RECEIVE

When you ***ASK*** for what you want, you're basically placing an order, just like on Amazon.com. But you have to be clear in your mind what you want. To get clear on what you want, make a list. Take out a notepad and scribble down whatever it is you want to have, do, or be. Whether that's perfect health, great relationships, an awesome career, travel, or peace on Earth and goodwill to all men. Whatever you're hanging out waiting for. Just be clear in your mind what it is you want, because a confused mind creates a confusing order. And a confusing order could see Amazon.com accidentally sending you Timbaland instead of Timberlake.

After making your order, it's important to ***BELIEVE*** that it's coming your way. Because that energy of belief is a perfect match with your desire, allowing like to attract like.

How do you make yourself believe? Easy. You act as if you already have whatever it is you want. They say a belief is just a thought repeated over and over. So pretend your desires are already yours. Like:

- There is a totally cool car in my garage.
- I have a date with my crush on Saturday night.
- I sent a song I wrote to a big-time record producer...and he loves it.

The more you do this, the more you really will believe that you've already received. And that is the key to attracting your desire.

The final step in the creative process is to ***RECEIVE***. So relax, kick back, and feel fantastic. Feel the way you expect to feel when you finally do manage to get whatever it is you've been hanging out waiting for.

And once you manage that jumping-on-the-couch kind of feeling, you'll be in perfect sync with your desire. And in that state, you'll be primed and ready to take ACTION. That means simply taking the inspired steps required to RECEIVE your desire. Take the phone call, answer the door, sign for the package. Whatever it takes to secure what you're wanting. In other words, create the conditions and the space in your life so that you're in a perfect situation to RECEIVE your desire when it lands on your doorstep.

To break that all down, you ASK and BELIEVE via your thoughts. But you RECEIVE through your actions.

Still, a lot of people get confused by the role of ACTION in the creative process. They figure, "Surely I have to *do* something to force what I want to happen." But chances are, you're completely clueless about *what* to do. So you end up bouncing off the walls like you're on a Red Bull rush, with no direction and no idea. It's all too hard and you get nowhere fast. What you need to do is chill and get set for inspiration.

"I dream my painting, and then I paint my dream."
Vincent van Gogh - artist

When the opportunity presents itself and you get that impulse to act, that's when you're taking effective action, instinctive action, ***inspired*** action.

Some people struggle to tell the difference between inspired action and just "doing." The difference is when you're just doing, you feel tired, like it's hard work and you're exhausted, like you're swimming against a riptide. It's a total struggle.

On the other hand, inspired action is a breeze. It's nothing like work at all. It's intuitive and instinctive, like riding the crest of a perfect wave all the way to shore. That's the feeling of inspiration; it's effortless and easy - it feels like magic.

So trust your instincts. Whenever you have an intuitive or instinctive or inspired feeling, follow it, because that's the Universe inspiring you - it's the Universe moving you to receive exactly what you asked for.

Okay, so, that's the creative process - Ask, Believe, Receive. Seems easy enough, but for some the tricky bit is to believe that you can make it all happen for you. So practice on some small stuff. Try something you totally believe you can attract. Like a particular song playing on the radio, or a phone call from your best friend. Give it a go. And when you believe it's on its way, it will come.

Even though small stuff is good to start with, the truth is, size doesn't matter to the Universe. Regardless of what you want - big or small, expensive or hard to get - as long as you truly, faithfully and unwaveringly believe it's coming, the Universe delivers on time, every time.

REAL STORIES

Michael's Secret

When my grandpa was alive – well, he was really a father to me – he always told me that I can be and achieve anything I want in life, and it only knocked me when I was sixteen. I kept on saying to him, "Dad, I don't think I'm gonna make first-team rugby. Dad, I'm scared that I might not pass this term." And I kept on telling him I can't, I can't, I can't, until one day he said to me, " 'Impossible' is just a small word thrown around by big men who find it easier to live in the world that they have been given than to explore the possibilities they have to change it!!!" When he told me this, I was shocked and amazed. I didn't know what to say. I wanted to say something but couldn't find the words to express myself. I just gave him a hug and said, "Thanks, Dad."

The rest of the evening I lay in bed and thought about what he told me. The next morning I woke up with a smile and a new look on life. I was free – no doubts, no questions, just yes yes yes, I can I can I can.

From there it was all a breeze – I made first team rugby, hockey, athletics, and tennis, and was loved and trusted by all my teachers and friends. I excelled in class, and to put the cherry on top I was appointed head prefect of the school. At prize giving I was sportsman of the year for two years in a row, and I'm going to make this year my third. After seeing The Secret, I'm more determined to be the best that I can be, and better!!!!

Michael, age 17
Durban, South Africa

"Take the first step in faith. You don't have to see the whole staircase. Just take the first step."

Dr. Martin Luther King Jr. – spiritual leader, civil rights activist

THE SECRET 101

Okay, so you're chilling and ready for inspiration to strike, waiting for the intuition or the instinct to kick in. And in the meantime, you're wondering how to use ***THE SECRET*** to deal with the day ahead. That's the ideal time to get your shine on, to plan your day in advance, setting the forces of the Universe ahead of you. Whether you're at school or work, out and about, or at home, consider all the events you have coming up - a game, classes, friends to catch up with, maybe even a big test. Think about what's ahead, and then apply the three steps of the Creative Process.

For example, let's say you've got something stressful on the schedule, a great opportunity but kind of terrifying at the same time. Like auditioning for the school play. If you apply the Creative Process, it might look a little like this....

ASK

When you first heard about the open auditions and decided you might be into that - or maybe even earlier, when you first decided you wanted to try acting - that's when you ***ASK***ed for it. So that means you can stop stressing about the audition, because it's happening just for you, because you ***ASK***ed for it. And that allows you to move on to the next step.

BELIEVE

See yourself onstage. Imagine how that feels. How cool will it be to wear the costume? Imagine learning your lines. And rehearsing. Picture yourself performing in front of a full house. Of course it's a total breeze for you, like you were born for this. What are the other people in the cast like? No doubt, they're talented and friendly and supportive and very cool. Visualize the standing ovation you receive after each performance. Would this be the most fun you ever had?

RECEIVE

Feel really good, and the law of attraction will handle all the rest. And the best way to feel really good might be to imagine how you'll feel when you get the news - you landed the role, and you're part of the cast. What will you do? Holler and scream in triumph? Then do it now. Or maybe high-five the next person you see? Then do that. Or would you run out into the street and hug some random right there on the sidewalk? Well, if that's how you feel, why not?!

ACTION

The only action you need to take at this stage is the inspired kind. Avoid just "doing stuff" because you think it might help. In other words, don't shave your head or dye your hair bright pink to suit your character before you even get the part. But you can ensure that your phone is on and charged so the director or drama teacher can reach you to let you know you've been cast. And you can check your schedule to make sure you are available for rehearsals and performances for the whole season. That's how you create the conditions and the space to make your acting dream a reality.

So no matter what you have scheduled, you can totally paint your whole day just the way you want to see it and experience it. Just Ask, Believe, and take inspired actions to Receive your perfect day.

This is something that actor and producer Drew Barrymore does every single morning - she plans her whole day in her mind down to each specific detail, whether that's chillaxing in her pj's or nailing her lines on the set of *He's Just Not That Into You*. She believes it's the best way, in fact the only way, to start every day.

"If you're going to be alive and on this planet, you have to, like, suck the marrow out of every day and get the most out of it."
Drew Barrymore – actor

20/20 RE-VISION

There's also something you can do at the end of each day. Think back over the course of the day to some situation that didn't turn out the way you wanted. Consider how your vibe or your thoughts at the time affected the outcome.

Like, maybe you asked your parents if you could stay out late on Saturday night, but you expected them to say no, so you were totally primed for a fight. And that's exactly what you got. Screaming, slamming doors, getting grounded, the works.

Now consider how moments like this affect you and make you angry, pessimistic, and despondent. But just before you fall into a funk, consider that you can flip the script on the memory and rearrange it in your mind. Revise, fantasize, improvise, make it up as you go along, but change the memory to an outcome you prefer. Give yourself a Hollywood ending, a happily ever after.

In the case of staying out on Saturday night, imagine you went into the discussion optimistically, with a calm, persuasive case, promising you'll call frequently, and that you'll be with responsible friends that your parents know and trust. Imagine them responding reasonably, you compromise on curfew, and everyone is happy.

Doesn't that make you feel better? Now, whenever you recall that situation, you'll think of the new, improved, happy ending instead of the argument. And this "director's cut" ending reinforces a better mood and happier thoughts, and that, of course, attracts better things in the future.

You can pull this revision trick anytime you're feeling a little played, if you've had a shocking day, or if you're totally up against it. That night, before you go to sleep, reflect back on the events of the day. Switch things up to suit yourself, raise your vibe, then sleep satisfied. And this is how to use ***THE SECRET***!

REAL STORIES

Michael's Secret

During my freshman year at this magnet high school, I was struggling miserably. I had an F, a D, and more bad grades on my marking period 2 report card. I had a horrible fear of being asked to leave the school for my terrible grades. This was the time that I found The Secret DVD, and it changed my life. I took my wretched report card and made an imitation of it on an Excel spreadsheet. I made all of the grades A's and had nice comments on my behavior.

Marking period 3, I was on the honor roll – I had better grades than I had in MIDDLE SCHOOL! This was meant to be! Now I'm halfway through marking period 2, sophomore year. Last marking period I received six A's and two B's and a slew of compliments on my behavior. All of my teachers are kind and thoughtful, I no longer struggle with classes, and I have never felt so good in my life. THANK YOU SO MUCH!

Michael, age 15
New Jersey, USA

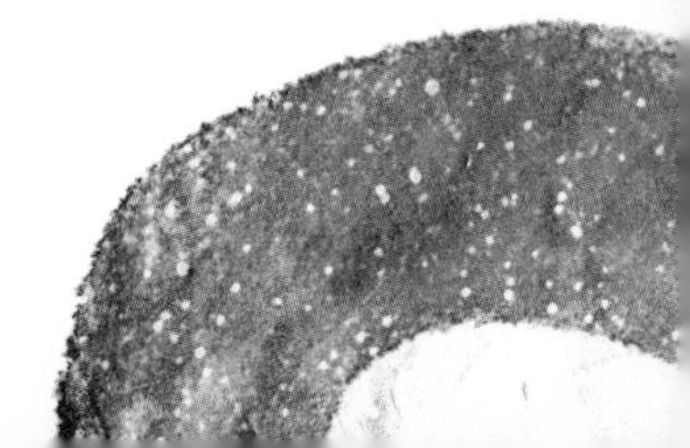

POWERFUL PROCESSES

SECRET POWER PLAYS

For some people, achieving the life of their dreams can take a lifetime to achieve. But it doesn't have to be that way. And if that's your angle, you'll be looking for a way to speed things up a little. Here are a couple of powerful tools to help you on your way.

GRATITUDE

All right, so you want it all, but when is the last time you said "thank you"? Not just some careless "thanks" to the juice bar counter clerk, but a real, genuine, heartfelt *thank you*? Probably don't remember, right? And that's a problem. Because that means you're not grateful, not really. Not to your parents, teachers, classmates, coworkers, or even best friends.

Saying please and thank you is so not cool, right? Like, it takes such an effort to be grateful. We whine about what we *don't* have, and by extension, we're not grateful for what we *do* have. We take everything for granted.

And taking what you have for granted is kind of messed up. It's impossible to bring more into your life if you're feeling ungrateful for what you *do* have. Why? Because the thoughts and feelings you send out when you're ungrateful are all negative vibes. Whether it's jealousy, resentment, frustration, anger, or whatever, those feelings aren't bringing you what you want. Those feelings and thoughts and attitudes just make you more depressed and miserable, and so of course they're attracting even more situations to make you feel depressed and miserable.

THE GRATEFUL PANTS

It's like in that movie *The Sisterhood of the Traveling Pants*. Four best friends are all focused on stuff they don't have: absent father, absent mother, absent romance, absent self-esteem. One of the girls, Tibby, the cynical emo type, has lost all hope and aspiration. So of course she attracts something that really is a downer – a terminally ill kid who just wants her life to matter. With her last breath, this little kid teaches Tibby and her friends that they have plenty to be grateful for – they have each other. And that's a great start.

REAL STORIES

Elizabeth's Secret

I can't really explain it. I had wanted to understand what Rhonda and the other great minds in The Secret meant by being grateful for everything you have and for everything you want. I wasn't sure I was able to do it. I've wanted so desperately to try to understand what it says, and manifest my own destiny. I didn't realize you couldn't receive anything until you were grateful for what you already have and what you will be receiving.

My understanding of gratitude began when I woke up to my alarm clock and was a little frustrated that I had to wake up so early. Immediately I changed my mood to one of happiness, and got out of bed. I was walking in the garden and began to feel the wind against my face, the grass between my feet, and I began to say thank you.

I got an emotion inside of me, one of completeness and of being whole. I began to truly feel grateful for what surrounds me; for my family, for my belongings, for my pets, for my clothes, for the Universe bringing back into my life the guy who I want to date (we finally talked after losing contact for six months! It is a miracle in my mind), and for everything. I didn't have to stop what I was doing and thank the Universe for what I have or what I want . . . no. Instead, I just felt this gratitude and happiness and love radiating out of me. It felt like magic, as if it almost wasn't possible to be so grateful. I could cry. I thank the Universe for what I want (as if it is already mine), for what I have, for what surrounds me.

I used to get angry very easily, but since discovering The Secret, and even more now that I am grateful for everything, very few things are able to upset me, and when they do I pull myself back and remember that only on a frequency of love, happiness, and gratitude will I receive what I want.

I only wish that everyone else will be inspired to truly be grateful for what they have and what they are receiving, because now I finally understand that once you are grateful for what surrounds you, you feel peace and love, inside which can only bring about what you want.

Elizabeth, age 19
California, USA

GRATITUDE GETS YOU GOOD STUFF

If you want to be happy and attract the life of your dreams, you've got to get grateful. Seriously. Being grateful shifts your whole energy and changes your thinking in a positive way. And remember, it's only when your thoughts are positive that you can attract good stuff into your life.

Let's say you want a new ride. In that situation, don't disrespect your current one. Even if it's just a ten-speed or a skateboard. Be grateful for all that it offers you: freedom, independence, and probably a heap of memories. And in that state of gratitude, that positive vibe, you'll be effortlessly attracting an E-Class ride.

Same goes if you're into clothes. Be grateful for the gear you're currently wearing, even if it is so last season. Just appreciate what you've got. Gratitude applies to everything you have, no matter how old or shabby. And when you *are* grateful for what you have, no doubt you'll attract the new Rip Curl, AE, Abercrombie, whatever, through the most unpredictable sources.

And if you still think it's uncool to say "thank you," then you'll just have to deal with the fact that your lack of gratitude is undermining your own dreams. It's not until you're absolutely grateful for all that you have and all you hope to have, that you can actually dial in your vibe to sync with your dreams and create that perfect attraction.

THE SECRET 101

To give your dreams a nudge, here's what you can do: write a list of things for which you are grateful. Write down at least seven items that you are thankful for every day. Think of it like your own personal "what's hot" list...all the stuff you own that you can look at and say, "Yeah, that's hot!"

Here are a few ideas to get you started:

- Clothes
- Music
- Movies
- Video games
- Books
- Cell phone/MP3 player
- Food

Whatever you can think of, write it all down. And it doesn't need to be just material objects. It can be people, too:

- Friends
- Family
- Parents
- Mentor
- Favorite teacher
- Girlfriend/boyfriend
- Best friend forever
- New relationships

Or things you love to do:

- Shopping
- Traveling
- Going to parties
- Hanging out with your besties

And what about good health? That's definitely something to be grateful for.

Whatever it is that makes you feel grateful, write it down. And remember, it's your "what's *hot*" list. Don't get distracted by "what's *not*." No need to be grateful that it's *not* raining or that you are *not* sick or that you're *not* lonely. Appreciate and give thanks for the great weather, your brilliant health, and all of your best friends forever. Because *that's* hot.

WISH LIST

You can also make this aspirational and intentional. That means you can use future gratitude to create an attraction for something you want, like a ***WISH LIST***. So let's say you've been hanging out for a new skateboard. You would say, "I am so grateful now that I have the perfect new deck." Make sure it's present tense - don't set this in the future or it will stay in the future. Don't be saying stuff like "I'm totally grateful for the new clothes/scooter/concert tix coming to me soon," because that just sets the clothes, the scooter, or the concert tickets on an eternal loop of coming soon. And you know how frustrating that can be.

Feel the gratitude of your ***WISH LIST*** as though you've already received it. Even if you don't have it yet and you have no idea how you're going to get your hands on it. Give no attention to that. Just say thanks for having it now.

So in addition to your seven aspects of gratitude, write down seven of these future aspirations.

Do this gratitude thing every day. Maybe set a time aside - first thing in the morning or late at night. And as you're writing down all this stuff, say the words "thank you." And feel the feeling deep in your heart; feel the emotions, and don't hold back.

And don't just leave your gratitude on the page - remember to share it with people. Because that's another great ***SECRET***: when you're grateful, and when you truly show your appreciation for people, they'll feel compelled to do more for you. It's the law of attraction at work once again, acting through them to bring you more of what you want. And all because you took the time to say thank you.

VISUALIZATION

Using ***THE SECRET*** to create your life is very much like making a movie of your life. ***YOU*** become the director, and ***YOU*** write the screenplay. But most important, ***YOU*** get to be the star. It's *your* movie, so whatever you do, don't become a background prop. Don't be an extra in your own life.

You can cast yourself in whatever role you want: superhero, romantic heroine, adventurer, or "it" girl.

YOU write the script; the scene is all yours to set.

And from the plot to the supporting cast to the locations to the production design to the action and of course the all-important wardrobe design, in every instance the first and most important step for you is to ***VISUALIZE***. In other words, imagine exactly what you want.

Imagine your life played out in high-definition. Whatever it is you want, imagine it... in pictures. See yourself doing it... in pictures.

And just like in the movies, those pictures evoke some pretty awesome feelings, which then create a vibe within you, resulting in the most powerful magnetic attraction. You totally transmit the picture with your thoughts, and the Universe picks up this transmission and beams it back to you in perfect clarity on a fifty-inch LCD screen. Except this home theater experience is actually your life happening all around you in 3-D. To make the experience even more real, you should add your other senses to the process. Include your hearing, smell, touch, and taste, and you create a multisensory experience, which makes this visualization even realer than real.

SEEING IS BELIEVING

The reason that visualization works so incredibly well is this: your mind naturally works in pictures, and the pictures you hold of yourself are very important. That's why they call it "self-image," because the images and pictures you hold of yourself are such an important, creative force. And when you deliberately create the pictures in your mind, you're transmitting really powerful, focused energy of actually being and becoming and having that experience. It's as though it's happening *now*. And the more vivid the pictures, the more convincingly you imagine it, the more real it will seem. And with that vibe you give off, the law of attraction can't tell the difference. You fool the Universe! Just like in the movies.

LIGHTS, CAMERA...ACTION!

Think of the last action movie you saw. Maybe there was an awesome chase scene or a spine-chilling ending. I bet your heart was racing - you were maybe even a little bit scared, amped up, or excited. Your body and mind reacted like the experience was real, as though it was happening to you. And that's what happens when you visualize: you ASK for the experience, your mind BELIEVES that it's real, and you radiate that thought out to the Universe, which creates the attraction for you to RECEIVE in your life.

This technique is favored by many of the world's great coaches and sports psychologists, as they encourage athletes to visualize the actual race or match or contest well ahead of time. Every stroke, every step, every leap, every muscle exertion vividly imagined. The idea is, when you see it in your mind, your body will surely follow. And, come the big day, mind and body are so well trained to act in unison that it becomes like second nature...and ultimate performance is virtually assured.

HEROES

Natalie Cook & Kerri Pottharst

To help visualize winning Olympic gold, Australian beach volleyball duo Natalie Cook and Kerri Pottharst took a very literal approach: they surrounded themselves with all things gold. They wore gold clothes and gold sunglasses, they bought gold cell phones and gold toothbrushes, and they especially favored those gold foil-wrapped chocolates in the shape of medals. They also placed the words to their national anthem all over their homes and practiced singing at every opportunity, because the national anthem always plays when you're presented with Olympic gold.

Cook and Pottharst won their way through to the final, and even though they may have been playing more talented opponents, their dreams of gold got them over the line. And as the medals were draped around their necks, they proudly belted out their national anthem just as they'd always imagined doing.

For Natalie Cook and Kerri Pottharst, the best and most effective way to visualize the ultimate was to literally surround themselves with the golden bling of victory. Now, whether you choose to imagine the end result, or to see every step along the path, either way, visualization is a terrific tool to help you go for your own gold.

Of course, you might not be an Olympic superstar (you may not even be the sporty type), but still, it's totally valid to visualize your dreams and desires as vividly as you possibly can. You have to be moved by the visualization; you have to see it and feel it powerfully, and you have to have an emotional attachment.

"Everything you can imagine is real."
Pablo Picasso – artist

PICTURE YOURSELF

Let's say you've got your eye on a new outfit. Go ahead and visualize that outfit. How does it look? Think about it for a few moments....

I bet you thought of your new outfit on a clothes rack in the store, on a mannequin in the window, or possibly in a photograph in a fashion magazine. But tell me, were you excited? Were you thrilled? Were you emotionally attached? Probably not. Because let's be honest, it's hard to feel that way about clothes racks and mannequins.

You've got to get yourself involved in the experience – put yourself in the picture. You need to imagine yourself active and in motion. It's no good just picturing a catalogue image, frozen and still; you'll never stay focused on a static photograph for long. To hold your attention, you need movement; you need full-motion video – a movie of you in your mind's eye. So visualize yourself in action, actually trying on this new outfit. Imagine how amazing you look in it. Notice how the color complements your eyes. How well you move in it. How it feels, the textures and the fabric. And how brilliantly you'll be able to accessorize it. Of course, it's a perfect fit.

So where are you going to wear your new outfit? To a party? On a date? Maybe to a club? Picture that. Imagine being escorted past the line at the velvet rope. All eyes are on you and your hot new outfit as you're welcomed into the VIP section. You meet many new and exciting people. You dance the night away in the arms of the hottest guy or girl. You have the time of your life. And as you make your way home somewhere around dawn, you think to yourself, "Could this possibly be the most perfect night and the most perfect outfit ever?"

THE SECRET 101

By now you should be able to see how powerful pictures are in the process of realizing your dreams. And in this process of creating the so-called movie of your life, you can draw some inspiration from the real-life dream-weavers - the movie makers of Tinseltown.

In planning their blockbuster hits, directors will often work with a production designer well ahead of shooting, to craft highly detailed illustrations and storyboards to demonstrate their intentions.

You can do something very similar and compile a Vision Board, a collage of images that represent all of your dreams and aspirations. Your Vision Board will help you focus on your desires, visualize them in your mind, and at the same time create a positive vibe. Your Vision Board acts as a constant reminder, providing evocative images of your dreams, and drawing your thoughts and your feelings together as a powerful force to attract your greatest desires.

To create a Vision Board, what you need to do is get a pair of scissors, and then raid your favorite glossy magazines and catalogues for pictures that evoke your dreams.

Here are some suggestions for images that might find a way onto your Vision Board:

- The college you're desperate to attend
- An amazing job making tons of money
- Front-row tix to the hottest band
- Meeting your favorite celeb
- A new boyfriend or girlfriend
- A hot body
- The latest styles, right out of *Project Runway*
- A brand-new car (or maybe a restored classic)
- The latest digital toy
- Traveling around the world

Once you have a selection of images nicely trimmed, you need to get your hands on a bulletin board and some pushpins. Or something you can tape your images to.

Arrange your pictures on the board according to your own creative impressions – there's no right or wrong. This is your chance to get creative. It's for no-one else's eyes but your own, so no need to be self-conscious. Get inspired, inventive, and artisitic; use your imagination, as well as any other skills you might be able to bring to the table.

REAL STORIES

Tien's Secret

I wanted to create several Vision Boards, but I was struggling with cutting images out of magazines because I had trouble finding pictures of exactly what I wanted. There were always pieces missing. The pictures never felt or looked quite right. So I thought about it, and came up with an even better idea.

I went online and found pictures of all of the things that I wanted to manifest in my life, and using Photoshop to edit and transform the images, placed things exactly where I wanted them to go. I created a total of eighteen Vision Boards! Not only that, but I used my digital camera to take pictures of myself "doing" and "having" and "being" all of the things in the pictures, and then cut myself out and added it to the boards. The end result is that they look AMAZING, and they are exactly what I want to manifest!

Not only that, one of the Vision Boards was of me rock climbing, something I've wanted to pursue for a long time but never had the opportunity. The day after I made that Vision Board, my boyfriend called me up and asked me if I wanted to go rock climbing with him and his best friend, because he'd only gone once and wanted to try it again! He didn't know I'd made the Vision Boards yet, either! We went, and it was a blast! I'm going again this weekend.

Happy manifestations, everyone!

Tien, age 19
California, USA

Now if, like Tien, you've got some Photoshop skills, you might consider creating your entire Vision Board digitally. Make good use of Google image searches as well as your digital camera. And don't forget to put yourself in the picture. You can then make your Vision Board the desktop wallpaper on your computer screen. Or you might like to upload it to your Facebook photo album, if you have one. Another cool thing you can do is turn some images into a slide show and make that your screen saver.

Either way, you will be able to see a snapshot of your dreams and aspirations at any time of the day or night. And this will help you visualize your way to a better life, tapping all the power of ***THE SECRET***.

THE SECRET TO MONEY

LIVING LARGE

Imagine you're Peter Jackson and you're directing some colossal epic like The Lord of the Rings. Then halfway through production, just as you're about to stage the major battle scene, the producer calls and tells you that you don't have the budget. Instead of ten thousand orc warriors, you only have four extras with crummy costumes and plastic swords. You planned an epic battle, but you're left with an epic failure. Whether you're making a Hollywood blockbuster or simply living your life, money does matter.

You might be thinking to yourself, "Hang on...what do I care about all that finance stuff? Leave the money worries until I'm old and crusty!"

Well, that's fair enough, but you know what? If you do think that way, chances are when you get to be old and crusty, you still won't have a decent handle on money. Suddenly it's like, forget ten thousand orcs and a Hollywood blockbuster...you won't even have enough money to buy a discount movie ticket.

So why not use ***THE SECRET*** to cash in *now* and be a step ahead for the rest of your life? Sound good? Of course it does. Because when you know ***THE SECRET***, you can attract all the money you need to have, do, or be anything you want, for as long as you want.

"Money is not the only answer, but it makes a difference."
Barack Obama - *U.S. president*

SHOW ME THE MONEY

Okay, so . . . what's the deal with money? And exactly what does it mean to you?

Check this out: a twenty-dollar bill, to look at, is just a small rectangular piece of colored paper. Nothing to get too excited about. But this colored paper takes on value because it's a tool of exchange; you swap it for goods and services - the stuff you need and the things you like. And if you have enough of these bits of paper, then you can do anything you want in your life, *when* you want to do it. That's what freedom really is - to do what you want, when you want. Living life on your own terms.

"A man is a success if he gets up in the morning and goes to bed at night and in between does what he wants to do."
Bob Dylan - *singer, songwriter*

Think for just a moment about all the things you could do in your life with that sort of freedom:

- Travel the world in style
- Chill with your best friends somewhere fabulous, like Maui
- Surf the best breaks all summer long
- Study music, art, dance, or drama with a renowned master
- Record a CD with someone like Timbaland as producer
- Make a movie starring Robert Pattinson and Kristen Stewart
- Give away money to randoms on the street
- Help the poor or the underprivileged
- Support an entire community in a developing nation
- Dedicate your resources to support environmental causes

Whatever your passion, you can do and have and be and achieve all these great things and more - for yourself and for the world. And it's all possible thanks to the colored paper.

Now, as you know, the law of attraction means that the thoughts you're holding in your mind - positive or negative – will attract either positive or negative things into your life. And to attract awesome things to you, including money, you want to make sure that you're choosing positive thoughts and feelings about money.

THE ROOT OF ALL EVIL?

Trouble is, a lot of people have this idea that money is responsible for all the bad stuff in the world. They convince themselves that money is the root of all evil, and that money corrupts.

People who think like this get to a point of hating on money like it's all about Wall Street suits getting rich off the poor. They trash the wealthy and refer to them as filthy rich. And it doesn't help that rich people always seem to be cast as villains on the screen. Think of Monty Burns from *The Simpsons* or Cruella de Vil or Kate Winslet's fiancé in *Titanic*.

But that's not the way it really is.

Check out Microsoft's Bill Gates, and Richard Branson, the founder of Virgin. Those guys seriously pay like they weigh; they've coughed up something like eleventy billion dollars to help the poor and improve literacy and education. So there are some decent causes right there. Fact is, while these two eccentric billionaires are super generous, they couldn't have done any of it if they were broke. Obviously. Like, how can you help the poor by joining their ranks? On the other hand, you can do seriously awesome things, for yourself and for the world, once you have the cash. And you can only attract it if you think positively about it.

TRUMP THIS

So, now that you know money is not about getting all Donald Trump and firing people, you can turn your attention to all the sweet stuff you want to attract into your life - all the things that make you feel good, all the things that money can bring you. Because people who draw serious money think just like that. They think thoughts of abundance and wealth, whether consciously or subconsciously, and they don't allow any contradicting thoughts of lack or limitation or there not being enough to go around. People with money control 85 percent of the world's wealth, yet they make up less than 10 percent of the world's population. And guess what? They know ***THE SECRET***.

Well, now *you* know ***THE SECRET***, and it's up to you how you use it. You can sit back and complain about the unfairness of it all and hate on money and never attract your own stack. Or you can step up and *add* to the world, create your own abundance, and become the top-billed box-office superstar in the blockbuster movie of your life.

HEROES

A Broke Actor's Dream

An out-of-work and broke actor once drove to the top of a hill that overlooks Hollywood, the city of stars. As he gazed over the movie lots, he reminisced about his hard life as a teenager, when he went to high school in the daytime and then worked as a janitor in a factory at night. Then there was the time his family was forced from their home and had to live out of a VW camper van. He refocused his attention into the present moment and then did something really provocative: he wrote himself a check for ten million dollars! On it he wrote, "For services rendered as an actor" and forward-dated it five years. He then carried that check with him everywhere to remind himself of his goal, and he simply got on with doing what he loved most – acting!

Five years later, on the very date that he had written on his check, that young actor was earning well beyond ten million for each film that he starred in. And the name on that check? Jim Carrey.

When Jim Carrey was broke and out of work, he had no reason to think he would earn $10 million! But he didn't let that stop him. He decided what he wanted and then believed he would get it. And you can do the same.

TELL ME WHAT YOU WANT, WHAT YOU REALLY, REALLY WANT

Put some thought into what you want in your life, financially speaking. Then visualize that you already have it, take the feelings your visualization brings up in you - any feelings of joy, gratitude, and happiness - and radiate them out into the Universe. This is the fastest way to bring wealth, happiness, and anything else that you want into your life. And as you do this, remember that it's not your job to know *how* all this money will come to you - just hold the faith that it *will* come.

Now get out and do more of the things in your life that make you feel good! Because therein lies yet another secret behind ***THE SECRET***...that money may not buy happiness, but it seems happiness *can* buy money. More or less. See, if you focus on doing more of the things that make you happy, then money is much more likely to be attracted to you. So fill your days with happiness and passion, and live this passion in everything you do.

"Passion is energy. Feel the power that comes from focusing on what excites you."

Oprah Winfrey – talk show host, producer, publisher

MONEY DOES GROW ON TREES

If you see that you're not happy with your financial picture, don't sweat it; just do your best and be all you can be. There are plenty of ways to make money, especially if you're prepared to step up and have an attitude of gratitude. Once you do, chances are you will attract attention. That is to say, you'll attract the right people and circumstances to help you attain all the opportunities, resources, and money you desire.

Qualifications, skills, experience, and an iPod touch full of good contacts might be beyond you right now, but passion, intensity, and a captivating charm are priceless in any situation. That is well within your grasp.

If you whine about stuff and tell everyone how unfair life is, exactly how does that help you get where you want to be? It doesn't. Nobody wants a whiner. So unless you have a real-life fairy godmother, you're not going to be whisked away in a horse-drawn pumpkin.

On the other hand, there are stacks of stories of young people plucked from obscurity by some rich benefactor because of their enthusiasm and their energy and their ambition to succeed. So no matter if you're flipping burgers or washing dishes or working the register at a convenience store, you should aim to be the best darn burger flipper, dish washer, or convenience store clerk that you possibly can be. Because you never know when Steve Jobs might walk through your door. Of course, the reverse is also true, and it may well be the very next door *you* walk through makes your dream job a reality.

HEROES

Steven Spielberg

Legend has it that as a young man, master filmmaker Steven Spielberg didn't wait for opportunity to knock... he knocked the door down himself. As a recent film school graduate, Spielberg wasn't content with dreaming of what it would be like working for a Hollywood studio; he went to see for himself. And after taking the standard Universal Studios back lot tour, Spielberg was eager to experience much more.

He noticed that all the Universal executives looked more or less the same – business suits and briefcases. So he got himself a new briefcase and a jacket and tie, and he marched right on through the front gate, waving to security as he passed by. He then found an empty office and made himself at home. And so with full access to all the soundstages and film sets, Spielberg was able to sit back in a canvas director's chair and watch and learn from the best. He visualized himself at the helm, making blockbuster movies with some of the world's biggest stars.

Several weeks into the scam, Spielberg got collared by a payroll clerk. But the studio didn't evict him on the spot. Like most of the Hollywood people who heard the story, the Universal suits were impressed by his audacity, and they offered him a paying job and a bigger office. And before too long, Spielberg was the youngest director in town, thanks to his enthusiasm, his passion, and his incredibly cunning plan.

"I dream for a living."
Steven Spielberg – *movie maker*

A TICKET TO RIDE

Okay, so maybe movie studios have tightened security a bit since way back when. And maybe making movies isn't your thing anyway. But still, you've got to get out there and get your name in lights, figuratively speaking. Be passionate. Be enthusiastic. Seek out the things you're totally into, that you love to do. And know that you can have it all: a great career, all the money you need, a cool place to live...everything you can think of.

The truth is, there's enough opportunity, money, resources, and abundance on the planet for you and for everyone. Know in your heart that anything you do want for yourself is possible. Choose to feel great and think abundant thoughts. Because your mind is your biggest asset when it comes to attracting as much wealth as you need to live the life of your dreams, do what you love, and love what you do.

THE SECRET 101

Take Jim Carrey's lead and write yourself out a million-dollar check. First go to

www.thesecret.tv/secretcheck.pdf

to download the dummy blank check. Print it out and write the check out to yourself. Fill in an amount you believe you might comfortably receive sometime soon. Date the check.

Now place that check somewhere you'll see it often. It could be on your mirror, or it could be in your wallet or bag. And don't try to do the math on how you might come by that amount of cash. That's not your purpose. You just have to believe and feel good, and get in sync with the idea that you can have, do, or be whatever you choose. That way the Universe will conspire and bring together people, circumstances, and events to deliver all that you wish for.

You can also turbo-charge your million-dollar intention if you like - just use some of these techniques explained earlier. . . .

GRATITUDE

Feel thankful for the abundance and prosperity that is inevitably flowing your way. Try a little future gratitude. Just be sure you set it in the present tense: "I am so happy and grateful for my affluence and good fortune."

And in feeling that gratitude, you shouldn't pause to concern yourself with how long the money takes to arrive or how you're going to get it.

VISUALIZATION

As you know, money itself is just colored bits of paper. So it's pretty hard to visualize these colored bits of paper and work up much excitement. What *you* can do is picture yourself enjoying the lifestyle and freedom that wealth affords you. Imagine what you will buy with unlimited money. Surround yourself with pictures of things you'd like. Feel the excitement of having those things and sharing them with the people you love. Because that's the coolest thing about having money: giving and sharing the love.

Once you achieve that feeling on a consistent basis - that feeling of having and giving and providing instead of going without - then you are in the vibe of money. And then you will never again have a budget shortfall in your life.

One last point when it comes to money: Bill Gates and Richard Branson were mentioned earlier, specifically their generosity and the billions they give away, or "tithe," as the practice is sometimes known. The word "tithe" means "tenth," and the tradition says you're supposed to cough up ten percent of your income for charitable purposes. Now, that might seem like a stretch, especially if you're not exactly flush with money. But check this out....

There's this school of thought springing from the mystical traditions of Jewish Kabbalah, and totally in sync with the law of attraction, that says that whatever you put out will be returned to you tenfold. Pretty cool side effect, huh? What you give, you get back multiplied.

> *"When you are kind to someone in trouble, you hope they'll remember and be kind to someone else. And it will become like wildfire."*
> Whoopi Goldberg – actor, comedian

REAL STORIES

Asher's Secret

I read about this "lucky bucks" idea on the internet and I decided to give it a try. What you do is you take a $5 note (or whatever is the smallest note you can get) and you write "Good Luck" or some other positive message in permanent marker. Then you stick it somewhere obvious where someone will find it. You can put it anywhere you like, but the only rule is, you're not supposed to stay to see who finds it. It is a random act of kindness, kind of like karma on My Name Is Earl – if you do good, then good comes back to you.

Anyway, me and my two friends went to the city with a stack of lucky bucks, and we stuck them in various places such as...

- *On the ceiling of a train*
- *On a pillar at the train station*
- *Inside a newspaper at the 7-Eleven*
- *Inside a birthday card at a newsagent*
- *On a pacifier packet in a grocery store*
- *On the door of a public restroom*
- *Inside a phone booth*
- *Inside a napkin dispenser*

I imagine that finding even small amounts of money in a place you wouldn't expect would really make your day, maybe even turn a bad day around. From my point of view, I am looking forward to the good luck to come to me, but I had a lot of fun hiding the lucky bucks.

Asher, age 15
Victoria, Australia

THE SECRET TO RELATIONSHIPS

HOOKING UP AND HANGING OUT

Whether we like to admit it or not, most of us want love and respect from everyone around us. It's all about that tribal vibe, that feeling of fitting in, of belonging, of being appreciated and loved.

But for many people, reality strikes and life doesn't always play out the way we might have hoped.

Have you ever felt misunderstood and all alone?

And are there moments when you say to yourself, "Why doesn't anyone *get* me?"

And does it sometimes seem like your parents have no clue about the problems you're dealing with?

And does it get to the point where you think you could just bail out and no-one would notice?

Sadly, many people feel that way. Maybe you do right now, or maybe you have in the past.

But now that you know ***THE SECRET***, you can totally flip the script, tapping the law of attraction to attract new and more exciting relationships. And you can also heal and rebuild existing relationships – even the ones that have blown apart or drifted away.

Truth is, your relationships either work or don't work because of one major reason: the thoughts that you hold in your head.

WHAT WERE YOU THINKING?

Did you ever notice that when someone rubs you the wrong way, it's just too easy to get caught up in the blame game? You point out what the other guy did wrong – how *he* messed up. Truth is, you should be pointing the finger at you. Sure, *he* might have done something uncool, but ask yourself, what did *you* do to attract this scene and this behavior?

What were *you* thinking?

Because that's what everyone else is responding to. And that's what you're attracting.

It's true for every relationship – with parents, teachers, your so-called friends, or anyone who's giving you a hard time. They're all responding to your vibe and giving you back what *you're* attracting.

So be aware, if you've got a messed-up relationship in your life, then there must be something messed up in the way you're thinking.

For instance, let's say you're looking for love and respect but you've got some issues with low self-esteem. In that case, you're projecting a vibe that says, "I'm unworthy of love and undeserving of respect." And guess what you're attracting?

Not love and respect, that's for sure.

SEE YOURSELF AS GARBAGE, AND THE FLIES WILL COME

When we're feeling disrespected, unloved, and miserable, it's normally a one-way ticket to Lonely Street. I mean, who likes to be around anyone who's miserable? You'd think no-one, right? Wrong! Other miserable people do...because misery loves company.

Remember, the law of attraction is always working, so when we feel sorry for ourselves, we attract other downers who are feeling sorry for *themselves*. People who whine about stuff love nothing more than finding others to have a pity-party with.

You have to get out of these situations as quickly as possible because you can never change anything by complaining. In fact, you simply get more of the stuff that you're complaining about!

So the first step is to change your tune - quit the drama and stop spreading your own misery. As for your pity-party pals: they're not helping you and you can't help them. Well, not unless you're a qualified emo-therapist.

PHYSICIAN, HEAL THYSELF

Speaking of therapy, you're the only one who can heal your own issues with self-esteem. Shift your focus to feeling good within yourself, and you'll naturally attract positive people and positive relationships into your life. And you'll also be well on the way to attracting the love and respect you're craving.

HEROES

Leisel Jones

Leisel Jones was a precocious fifteen-year-old when she burst onto the world stage, winning a silver medal at the 2000 Olympics in Sydney. Having been crowned the new teen idol of swimming, the pressure was on when Leisel came back to compete in Athens four years later. But in Athens she struggled to earn a bronze medal and didn't do a very good job hiding her disappointment. Unfortunately, the media and the general public took notice, criticizing her for being immature and ungrateful.

What no-one knew was that Leisel was totally distraught by her loss. She felt she had let everyone down, especially her single mom, who'd literally given up everything for Liesel. With her dreams in ruins, she was emotionally ravaged.

Leisel grew up in the public eye with no time for friendships or dating, and like many teens, she also had low

> *self-esteem. She ended up shutting herself off and considered quitting her sport. As she said, "It got pretty dark." Eventually Leisel knew something had to give. She came to realize she needed to learn to love herself before anyone else could.*
>
> *And so from the depths of depression and despair, Liesel Jones re-emerged. While it was hard work getting there, within twelve months she had completely turned her life around. And now that she had come to love herself, others started to love her too. She finally had her first steady boyfriend, sponsors were climbing on board, and even the public had forgiven her.*
>
> *And then there was her swimming; faster, stronger, self-confident, and determined, Leisel Jones smashed several world records on her way to accomplishing her life's dream – a gold medal at the 2008 Beijing Olympics. And she attracted it all by generating thoughts of love within.*

It makes perfect sense if you think about it – to find love and earn respect, you have to *be* love and *be* respect. You've got to feel it within yourself before others feel it for you.

Okay, so now you know that feeling good is the key to love, respect, and great relationships. But you may be thinking, "Yeah, right. Easier said than done."

Well, it all starts with just one positive thought of love and respect for yourself. It could be something as simple as:

- I've got a wicked sense of humor.
- I'm smart and thoughtful.
- I have a unique perspective on the world.
- I'm witty and fun to be around.
- I'm a great listener.
- I'm a loyal, stand-up kind of friend.

Dig deep and find the one thought that resonates with you, that feels true to you. Focus on that thought, and then say it to yourself in the morning when you wake up, at night right before you go to sleep, and many times in between. As you do, the law of attraction will start showing you even *more* cool things about you, because you'll be attracting more of what you're thinking about. You'll attract more "like" thoughts and stronger feelings, and before you know it, you'll be so self-assured you could tutor Will Smith on confidence!

SEEK AND YE SHALL FIND!

Self-confidence is just filling yourself up with love and feeling good about *you*. Want proof? Check it out....

You may have noticed at every party, gathering, or social situation you're in, that the most confident guy in the room is surrounded by girls *and* guys the minute he walks in the door. Why is that? It's because he projects cool; he feels good within himself. He's having fun, and, most important, he's fun to be around. So he attracts a crowd – it's magnetic.

But how did this guy get so confident? Well, no doubt he would have started with just one good thought about himself, and it grew from there. As for all the guys and girls surrounding him, they're all attracted by his confidence, charisma, and self-respect. Don't you see, they love him because *he* loves him.

And this is one of the biggest secrets of the lot. Most people think happiness and being cool comes from the love and respect of others. They seek out love and respect to make themselves happy and to feel cool. But that's backward. You make *yourself* happy, and that attracts love and respect. Look for the positives inside you and focus on those things with appreciation, and then radiate that vibe. Then step back and feel the love.

REAL STORIES

Cassie's Secret

I lived with my mom until I was twelve years old, and that is pretty much where it all started – my problems with my low confidence and self-esteem. I remember my mom always saying how fat she thought she was, even though she was stick-thin and hardly ever ate.

A couple of years ago I was forced to move to my dad's house because of my mom's personal problems. I have struggled for the past few years with my own eating habits, even though I have been in such a healthy environment living with my father.

I read The Secret about a year ago but somehow did not fully absorb it, because I continued to struggle. A few months ago my dad and I visited a therapist to try to help with my near constant sadness and low self-esteem. It has helped somewhat, but not until I read The Secret again did I truly begin to love myself.

I've realized that I am beautiful and perfect as I am. I've tried to show my now recovering mom the miracle of learning The Secret, and how it could help her, but she doesn't seem to care. But one day I know she will see how beautiful she is too. Although it's hard sometimes, I do my absolute best to stay positive every day, and will continue to use The Secret in my life.

You must learn to love yourself before you can truly love anyone else.

Cassie, age 16
Michigan, USA

"To love oneself is the beginning of a lifelong romance."
Oscar Wilde – playwright, poet, author

When you love yourself, you automatically attract feelings of love for others around you. And likewise, when you love others, that attracts feelings of love from them toward you. Your love for yourself literally attracts love from others; it gives them reason to love you.

On the other hand, if you're determined to project an image of self-loathing, that's all people see. And to be completely honest, self-loathing isn't so lovable. Especially if thick eyeliner and black sweaters don't suit you.

So focus instead on the positive aspects of who you really are. Stick yourself on a pedestal, smile for a change, and let your unique bent, your warmth, and your humor light up the world.

A word of caution: your old pity-party pals who aren't used to this new you might take awhile to get it. Some may never. They may even get mad that you're no longer miserable, self-loathing, and whining.

And you know what? That's okay. People change. Sometimes they drift apart. If that happens, it needn't be a sad thing. Just know that friends sometimes drift away to make space for others to come into your life. And for sure these new friends will be totally in tune with the new, happy you.

Of course, the law of attraction doesn't work just on your relationships with friends and family; it can also give your romantic life a serious boost. How? You guessed it – through the power of your thoughts.

YOU HAD ME AT "HELLO"

Have you ever had a total crush on someone but were too afraid to ever do anything about it, to take the first step or to make the first move? Maybe you were scared of what might (or might not) happen when others found out about your feelings. Maybe you were worried that you weren't good enough or that you'd look kind of stupid.

I bet you've been there, right? Everyone's been there. It's like you turned into Tobey Maguire's character from the movie Spider-Man – terrified of the consequences of asking his crush, Kirsten Dunst, on a date (and totally clueless to the fact that she's kind of into him, too).

But why? Why are people so afraid to take a chance? Usually it's because they don't feel worthy or they're scared they'll be rejected. Fair enough; who likes rejection? No one. But if that's what you're thinking, then welcome to Rejectville, population: you.

DESPERATION IS DATE REPELLENT

On the other hand, let's say you do build up the courage to overcome the fear of rejection. Then, as you approach your new crush, you're probably nervous and sweating and shaking and stammering. Let's face it, you look desperate. And as everybody knows, desperation is "date repellent." Your crush may not be able to put his or her finger on what it is, but their instinct will scream out,

"Avoid at all costs - weird emotional baggage."

So what you need to do is this: instead of rejection, think affection, think selection, think a change of direction, and, above all, think perfection.

Change your thoughts and realize that you deserve the attention of this person. Then visualize yourself out with him or her, having a great time, laughing and enjoying each other's company. See the end result that you want *first* and then take the plunge!

If it's meant to happen, then it will happen. Best-case scenario, you end up madly in love in a Hollywood-style happily ever after. And if not, don't stress. If it's not quite happening for you when you're in this state of mind, it's because the Universe has something better cooked up. And no doubt other great opportunities will be coming your way now that you've elevated your thinking. You're no longer buried in gloomy thoughts of rejection; you're all about affection, selection, a new direction, and perfection. So crush or no crush, something hot is bound to happen for you.

HE'S JUST NOT THAT INTO YOU

Now, that last part might feel like it's a bit hard to take, especially if you've got the dreaded One-itis (that is, when you're obsessing on someone in particular). And if you're in this situation, you might be confused over why you can't use ***THE SECRET*** to win your heart's desire. You might even be thinking the law of attraction has failed you, or there's some kind of flaw with the law. After all, ***THE SECRET*** tells us that what you think about, you bring about, right?

Okay, what you have to remember is that you can only control your own thinking and your own feelings. You can't control the thoughts or feelings of others. Seriously, this is not *Star Wars*.... ***THE SECRET*** is no Jedi mind control. You can't make anyone do anything - like fall in love with you - against their will.

It's just like in Disney's *Aladdin* when Genie explains the rules about the three wishes. Remember? He says you can't force someone to fall in love with you. Well, whoever wrote that really knew about the law of attraction, because it's the exact same deal in life: you can't force someone to fall for you against their own free will.

Think about it: What's your real desire? What's your wish? Is it love and romance? Do you want to find your perfect match? Or do you want to hook up with a particular person, even if that means being with someone who just isn't that into you?

How do you think that would turn out? Resentment, a messy breakup, and heartache guaranteed. That's not what you want. You want love and romance, but also happiness. You want your *perfect* match.

So try forgetting about anyone specific for a moment. In fact, don't think of anyone you know, or anyone you don't know. Don't even think about people. Instead, focus on a feeling, a vibe of your *ideal* hookup, your ultimate date. Just imagine how that experience would be - your senses, your heartbeat, how it would feel.

Who knows, you might end up with that crush of yours. Or maybe there's someone else you know who's perfect for you, only you never thought of that person like that before. Or maybe there's someone even better about to walk into your life.

Trust that the Universe will come through for you. Put the right vibe out there and allow the ideal attraction to come... *whoever* that may be.

THE SECRET 101

When scriptwriters write romance, their greatest challenge is to create compatible characters - the perfect match. So they spend a ton of time fleshing out these characters by describing who they are, where they come from, what they're into, and so on. And you can cast your own romance by doing the exact same thing.

ASK

Grab your notebook and take a few minutes to describe *your* perfect match. Hold an image of this future "soul mate" in your head and start writing. Get as detailed as you like - whether you write a few sentences or a couple of pages is completely up to you. But don't forget, the point is to steer clear of describing an actual real-live crush by thinking about the "who." That's not your job right now. Instead, focus on your "type," and what they're like and what they're into.

You can describe physical details if you want: hair color, eyes, skin, height, weight, measurements. It's your call. But don't get stuck just on the physical - personality is also key. And common interests are essential. Remember, you're casting your perfect match.

Here are some ideas for the kinds of details you might want to think about:

- Sense of humor
- Intelligence
- Athleticism
- Fashion sense
- Hobbies
- Volunteer interests
- Taste in music
- Favorite movies

Done? Great!

Now that you've got a description, it's time to feel the vibe of what you described on an *emotional* level... like you and your brand-new soul mate have already met and you're totally into each other. How would that feel? Close your eyes and totally feel the excitement of connecting with this dream date/soul mate. Feel it in your heart. Feel the warm fuzzies.

BELIEVE

Put your attraction into action by writing about the things you imagine you and this person doing together: dancing, movies, walks on the beach, texting each other fifty times a day...whatever comes to mind. Don't forget to include lots of details, like how you relate to each other, how this person treats you, and how he or she makes you feel.

As you write out these scenes, visualize them happening and imagine the sights, the sounds, the smells, in fact, all the sensations. If you can make this a multisensory experience, feel it on so many levels and really plant that thought-belief in your mind, you're well on the way to making it come true.

RECEIVE

You might think it's a little strange to spend so much time describing a relationship you're not even in yet. Well, it might be strange, but it works! Writing about your ideal match will help you feel the feelings that go along with being in that perfect relationship. And if you can truly imagine these experiences in your heart and your mind, you'll start to project a whole different vibe. Keep it up, and you're sure to attract romance beyond your wildest dreams. And not just any romance...since you've cast the role to perfection, you'll attract a match practically made in heaven.

CAST YOUR LIFE

This "casting" trick doesn't work for just romance. You can apply the same technique to all of your relationships, from family and friends to teachers and classmates, or even someone at school or work who's giving you grief. The only difference is, you are not actually recasting these roles; you're not necessarily looking to replace these people in your life. You're simply rewriting the way you choose to relate to them.

And that's crucial in all your relationships. No matter what anyone does to aggravate you, it's always your choice how you react. You can choose to get upset or you can brush it off. If you do choose anger, then ask yourself, "What is my next move?" Are you going to stay ticked off or are you going to get over it? Do you choose to focus on the bitterness or appreciate and be grateful for anything positive this person brings to you? It's your call.

The bottom line is simply this: relationships are all about relating.

SEVEN THINGS I ~~HATE~~ *LIKE* ABOUT YOU

So next time your parents give you a hard time, or a friend suddenly turns to the dark side, give them some space and try to relate – try to understand the situation from their perspective. Then put pen to paper and write out any positive thoughts you can come up with about the person. This is like the exact opposite of a burn book - you're filling it with *good* thoughts.

Sure, thinking good thoughts about someone who's making your life miserable is easier said than done. So start small. Try writing down seven things you fully appreciate about this person. (You might need to be creative, but you can do it.) Do this for a few days in a row, and genuinely *feel* the appreciation and gratitude as you do it, and the relationship will change before your eyes.

REAL STORIES

Jason's Secret

I have gone through a really rough and busy year. There has been a lot of stuff being said about me, and there was this one guy who seemed to have a mission to make me miserable. He seemed to be going out of his way to make me miserable!

I found out about The Secret and read the book first, and then watched the movie. I started sharing The Secret with my friends, family, and teachers.

My main goal was to simply be happy at school. According to The Secret, all I had to do was see it, and then have it.

I started visualizing myself being popular at school, having great relationships with my friends, and not being accosted or confronted by anyone.

Amazingly, everyone is being nice to me now, and even my enemy has turned! This is how it happened. . . .

He was sitting with a whole lot of his mates, and I had to get past. I expected the worst. Then I remembered what I had visualized. I walked past without a problem. On the way back past them, my enemy called me to him. I went to him and just hoped he wouldn't do anything bad. He started chatting to me as a mate! His mates started praising some of my achievements. It was awesome!

I attracted this and other things to me through the use of The Secret. You can begin NOW to change EVERY-THING.

MAKE YOUR LIFE WHAT YOU WANT TODAY!

Jason, age 15
Johannesburg, South Africa

At the end of the day, it's really quite simple. The key to success in any relationship is just to keep real, be true to yourself, and feel great. *That's it.* If you're doing that, then you can't help but project a positive, attractive vibe. You'll start to feel as though the entire Universe is doing everything for you, and that you're attracting cool people to you.

And, most likely, even your worst frenemies will get with it and find themselves on your side before they even know what's hit them. Don't believe it? Give it a try. You just might be amazed at how quickly change can happen.

So make it a goal to see the best in everyone, and the best will come back to you. By changing your thoughts, you have the power to change all your relationships, and you'll be all set to hook up, hang out, and have a better life. And that is ***THE SECRET***...to relationships.

THE SECRET TO HEALTH

WHAT'S UP, DOC?

Ever noticed how we're constantly bombarded with propaganda about our health and our body? This looks good, that doesn't look good; exercise this way, exercise that way; eat this, don't eat that. No wonder so many of us have issues!

But...that's exactly the point. All this pressure is nothing more than a slick marketing campaign designed to make us conform. The thing is, you're a work in progress, and no-one has the right to disrespect or criticize or judge you.

Seriously, can you imagine Will Wright, the dude who created The Sims, getting all heated just because someone from the beta test team posted a negative review of his latest, still-in-development game? Why would he stress about anything that interferes with his vibe? He's mega successful. And the new game isn't even finished.

Well, just like Will Wright, you're creating your own blockbuster. But of course, this isn't The Sims; it's no simulation and it's no game, it's ***YOU***. And, like Wright, you don't need to pay attention to the negative reviews about you. You don't need to read all those fashion mags implying that you look like you just walked off the set of *Ugly Betty*. Only read things that make you feel good,

and only do things that make you feel good, that make you feel *all that*, that make you feel great about yourself.

And you have to feel good about yourself. Because if you think of yourself as Ugly Betty, that's a powerful vibe, and you'll continue to attract ugly thoughts about your body. You'll never change if you're feeling unattractive and constantly criticizing and finding fault. In fact, you'll just attract more of what you're complaining about - too fat, too thin, too pale, too what*ever*. Chillax.

LOVE THE ONE YOU'RE WITH

Give yourself a little love and respect. Credit yourself for every square inch of your body. Strike up some positive affirmations. Try some of these on for size:

- "I see only perfection."
- "I have the ideal body type for me."
- "I am fit and healthy."
- "I am well cut."
- "I am strong."
- "I love my body as it is."

Or come up with your very own affirmations to make you feel good about the way you look.

Check out the movie *Hairspray*. That film is a classic challenge for the mainstream beauty myth. Notice how Tracy

Turnblad doesn't let her size distract her from her dream of becoming a TV dancer. She just gets on with dancing, letting her natural talent shine. And as she overcomes adversity, not to mention her thin and pretty rival, Amber, we come to see that beauty is not all about size 1. It's about what we think and feel on the inside.

"You can't stop my happiness, coz I like the way I am."
Edna Turnblad, in Hairspray

Same deal applies to guys. If you're looking in the mirror and you're hoping to see a Spartan warrior from *300* with ripped abs, buff pecs, and bulging biceps, you may be relieved to learn that those guys were all digitally enhanced. Yeah, wouldn't we all like our own personal digital enhancer?

The point is, having a six-pack stomach won't make you happy, even though you might think your flab or your scrawniness is making you unhappy. Happiness can only come from within you; it's an inside job. You attract happiness the same way you attract people, circumstances, and events – you attract by what's happening on the inside. Your magnetism comes from within.

Check this out: if you take a magnet and paint it some ugly color, that magnet wouldn't lose its properties; it would still attract. The magnetism doesn't come from the painted surface, it comes from the magnetic core. Same deal with you. It's nothing to do with being tan or having a great complexion or gorgeous, flowing hair. It's what's inside that attracts others to you. You've got to work on your magnetic core by being happy within.

So relax. Give your body a break and make the decision to be happy ***NOW***. You'll soon find that your inner magnetism is far more attractive than any bulging pecs or a gorgeous body. Besides which, if you don't have the personality or the charm or the happiness inside you, nobody's interested in what you look like in a swimsuit.

ON THE FACE OF IT

That's not to say that you can't change your appearance if you want to by using the power of your mind and the law of attraction. As an example, let's say you wanted to use ***THE SECRET*** to create great skin. Do you seriously believe you can change your complexion using the power of your thoughts? Of course you can. In fact, you've probably already done exactly that at some point, only in reverse.

Like when you have a sudden outbreak of acne just days before the school formal or prom, or anything major. Or maybe it didn't even start with you; maybe your besty had a zit right on the tip of his or her nose. You observed that, and maybe even teased your friend about it. And then suddenly, like some pimple epidemic, you score one of your own right in the middle of your forehead. It's the law of attraction summoning pimples to you.

So you start to obsess, and what happens? Your skin gets worse. And then you stress, and it gets worse still. By now you're possibly starting to suspect it was your obsession with these pimples that was actually feeding them all along. The law of attraction strikes again. But it stands to reason that if you can adversely affect your looks - if you can attract a major zit using ***THE SECRET*** - then you can also clear your skin using the same power of your mind. But how?

You have to break this cycle. Stop obsessing about what you don't want; stop obsessing about pimples. Just apply your cleansing and topical applications, and then leave your skin alone. Forget about it. See it as perfectly clean. Visualize it. Believe it. A concealer might be useful because it helps you believe. Be grateful for your clear skin. And give no more power or thought to bad skin. And if you can let go, and truly believe, you're bound to attract perfect, clear skin in no time.

REAL STORIES

Shannon's Secret

I love my sister and knew she could benefit from The Secret. But I was so hesitant to try to get into it with her because I knew she would be skeptical. Well, I started telling her about it anyways, and sure enough, she asked me if I was insane, ha-ha. But the more I talked about it, I think the more open to actually listening to me she became.

My sister has (had) really bad skin. She struggled with acne for ages. She was at my house one day and I realized why she had such a problem with her skin and self-esteem. She would look in the mirror and say, "Ugh, I hate my skin. It's so bad. Look at the bags under my eyes. I look horrible today. I feel horrible today." I told her, "Stop! You're making it worse. You're attracting all those things back to you, so they will never go away." Of course she was like, "Yeah, whatever, Shannon, blah blah blah." But I gave her a copy of The Secret audio book anyways (which is really good because she could never sit down and read anything other than Us Weekly).

She started to get jazzed about it and her attitude/way of thinking started to change. A week later she came over to my house and almost all of her acne was gone. I told her, "Oh my God, your skin looks so good!" And she said, "Thanks, I've been using The Secret to heal my skin."

Shannon
California, USA

THE SECRET 101

Like millions of people, you may already have a presence on internet forums and social networking websites such as Facebook, Twitter, and MySpace, as well as instant messaging or video chat services like Yahoo, Skype, and Windows Live. In which case, you'd know that these services allow some degree of personalization to let you more or less own the space.

For instance, you get to choose an avatar or an image that totally represents you online. Most people choose some generic picture from a clip art folder. But you have the opportunity to run with a custom-designed avatar that creates an *ideal* vision of you. And because it's the image that billions of people all around the interweb get to see of you, that means you're tapping some powerful vibes to help you visualize and create the perfect you.

Okay, so if you currently have a boring, generic online identity, it's time for an e-makeover. And the first step is to take a favorite scanned or digital picture of yourself and glam it up. Google "caricature avatar," and you'll find heaps of sites willing to take your face and turn you into some Amazon goddess, superhero, beauty queen, or ninja warrior in a range of artistic styles from airbrush fantasy, to DC comics, to anime, to *The Simpsons*, and many more. And, of course, they'll give you a killer body and maybe even place you in a setting of your choosing.

Apply this image to your MySpace, Yahoo, or Facebook page and follow it up with an online attitude of confidence and self-assurance to match your new self-image. And make sure your biography, personal interests, and status updates make no mention of downer moods or bad attitudes, and take care to avoid trolls and flame wars. Make your whole online persona a positive one because your online ID is at the forefront of your efforts to create a new identity, and ultimately unleash a brand-new you.

HEALTH BY STEALTH

Using the law of attraction, it is clearly possible to change aspects of your body and looks for better or for worse. And so it stands to reason, you can also apply this stuff to your health, as the medical masterminds are starting to figure out.

Consider this: every thought you have, and every emotion connected to that thought, releases chemicals throughout your body. Positive thoughts equal positive chemicals, which is like an incredible buzz. Negative thoughts equal negative chemicals, and that's more like a buzz-*kill*. You know of people who worried themselves sick, right? That's because when you continuously think negative thoughts, the stress creates negative chemicals in your body, and those negative chemicals actually affect your immune system. The inevitable result is that you attract disease and illness.

You see, illness comes from stress, and stress begins with one single negative thought. It might be something simple, like "It's flu season... hope I don't catch anything." Then, when that thought goes unchecked, another one develops, like "I'm feeling a little funky... better not have a cold." And then another thought: "How can I cram for my exams if I have a cold?" And then: "How can I pass my exams if I don't cram?" And finally: "How can I get into college if I flunk my exams?"

So one thought develops, and then more thoughts are attracted, and more, until stress surges through your body and manifests itself as illness. The effect is illness, but the cause is negative thinking and fear, and it all begins with one little thought. But of course, you can use this to your advantage, by choosing to focus on thoughts of perfect health. And you will attract perfect health.

DON'T AFFIRM THE GERM

Another thing that people do when they have an illness is talk about it with anyone who'll listen. They do it because they're *thinking* about it constantly - they're just verbalizing their thoughts. But here's the deal: if you're feeling like crud, don't talk about it unless you want more of it. Accept that your initial thoughts were largely responsible for attracting illness in the first place; okay, that was your mistake, but get over it, let it go. Then repeat this in your mind as often as you can: "I feel awesome. I feel totally fine," and really mean it. Really *feel* it.

If you're not doing so great health wise and somebody asks you how you're feeling, just keep it to yourself. Never, ever say "I'm sick." That's like defining who you are by sickness. It's like introducing yourself as your illness: "Hi, nice to meet you, I'm Strep Throat!"

That's not who you are. That's just how some part of you is feeling temporarily. Seriously, think of what that attracts when you say it out loud: "I am sick!" More sickness, that's what.

ALLERGIZE THIS

Allergies are much the same. A lot of people take on allergies like a new season's fashion. Every spring, a brand-new look. Except this look is kicked off by the radio weatherman telling you there's a high pollen count that day. And that's when your new look kicks in – bleary, puffy red eyes, sneezing and red-nosed with all sorts of nasty mucous. It's not exactly high fashion, is it?

So ignore allergy and illness and speak only the words of what you want. And then if anyone asks, "How are you doing?" You'll be like, "I'm awesome! I'm outstanding! Man, I'm living the dream!" Because that's where you want to be.

SPEAK TO THE HAND

One other thing: you can also invite illness if you're with a friend who's whining about their illness. As you listen, you're giving all of your thought and focus to their illness, and when you give all of your thought to something, you're asking for it. So guess what? You can attract their illness to you. And you're certainly not helping your friend, either – you're adding energy to their illness.

If you *really* want to help that person, change the dialogue to good stuff, healthy stuff, life-affirming stuff, well-being stuff. If you can. And if not, get out of there. As you walk away, give your powerful thoughts and feelings and your whole vibe to seeing your friend well - and then let it go.

"The secret of health for both mind and body is not to mourn for the past, nor to worry about the future, but to live the present moment wisely."
Buddha - spiritual teacher

DOCTOR KNOWS BEST

With medical knowledge where it's at these days, you'd be crazy not to take full advantage of all your doctor's advice, especially if you've attracted some funky disease into your body. However, every now and again, a case crops up that stumps the medical brainiacs, proving the immense power of mind over matter.

HEROES

Frank Capra

Back in Hollywood's golden era, renowned film director Frank Capra had just won his first Oscar but was stressed out of his mind about how to follow up and live up to all the hype and expectations. He really just wanted to quit and walk away, but he had a two-picture contract with Columbia Studios, so he had to deliver. Or did he? Capra schemed that if he got sick, they couldn't expect him to work. So that's what he did, faking illness, fooling the doctors, and staying home with his feet up. Of course, the studio and the doctors didn't give up on him. They ordered all manner of tests and came up with startling results: rapidly rising temperatures and an ominous spot on his lung. Capra was initially amused by the diagnosis – tuberculosis, or pneumonia, or some undiscovered malady. Capra's amusement turned to concern when he really did start feeling the effects of disease. It seemed that all these thoughts of illness were actually making him very ill, as he found himself bedridden and virtually at death's door.

Then one day Capra received a strange visit to his sickbed from a little man . . . someone he'd never met. He asked Capra to listen to Hitler's hate-filled ranting on the radio. Then he admonished Capra for not using his own voice to speak to the hundreds of millions of moviegoers who were inspired by his movies. It was a cowardly affront to God, or so the man said, that Capra was refusing to use his natural talent. Especially when the world really needed his brand of hope and wonder, what with all the misery and suffering and talk of a world war. Capra was shamed into action. He pulled himself out of bed and willed his recovery.

Frank Capra won his second Oscar within a year of his return, and a third two years later in the hottest streak of any filmmaker in the history of Hollywood. And he never missed another day from illness.

The point is, with the power of your mind, it's possible to make yourself chronically ill. But it's also possible to overcome disease. Frank Capra managed both.

If you're in this situation, or if you're genuinely ill, first up, you have to do the smart thing and get your doctor on the case. Let the medical scrubs do what they're going to do, while you accept your part in the deal. Realize that your own power to influence and even cure your condition rests in changing your thoughts right now. And anyone - no matter what state of chronic illness they've attracted - can choose to change their thoughts... ***NOW***.

Miracles happen; that's a fact. Don't believe me? Check this out:

- Champion cyclist Lance Armstrong was diagnosed with testicular cancer, which had spread to his lungs and brain. His doctor said he'd be lucky to live, let alone ever ride again. But Armstrong was determined to thrive, not just survive. He opted for radical treatment and intensive exercise that saw him back competing in just a few short months, culminating in seven consecutive Tour de France victories.

- Australian Rules footballer Jason McCartney was a victim of the 2002 Bali bomb attacks, suffering shrapnel wounds and third-degree burns to 50 percent of his body. McCartney was in a coma for a week and was offered last rites when doctors feared he may not survive the night. McCartney recovered and fulfilled his dream to marry his fiancée, just two months later, followed by a triumphant return to football the next season.

- Oscar and Emmy Award–winning actress Halle Berry was first diagnosed with diabetes after passing out on a film set. Berry was soon given the prognosis of a lifetime of insulin dependency. But through a strict combination of diet and lifestyle, Berry has the condition in check.

Sure, all these famous people had access to the best medical resources to help kick the conditions they were dealing with. But another vital resource was inside their head.

And it's the same for you. No matter what your condition, you have to be able to *imagine* your way to perfect health. Regardless of the disease that might have manifested in your body, regardless of the diagnosis, you can help change it — you can attract better health with the power of your mind, through consistent positive thoughts.

And with these consistent thoughts, you have to focus purely upon well-being. You can't be thinking of fighting disease or overcoming adversity or beating your condition. Because the law of attraction gives you exactly what you focus on: more of the fight, more of the disease, a worse condition.

THE PHYSICIAN HEALS; NATURE MAKES WELL

But again, that's not to say you can afford to disrespect the opinion of your doctors or reject medicine. Because mind and medicine, used together, are the most formidable method of healing - it's a team effort. Especially if you're struggling big-time, medicine can help you deal with the extremes of pain and other complications, the symptoms, and the side effects. Whether it's with medication, treatment, surgery, or whatever, medicine helps remove the distractions of illness so that you can do your job, which is focus your thoughts and energy on perfect health and well-being. And that allows your body to do just what it was designed to do - heal itself.

And straight up, it is as easy to cure a disease as it is to heal a pimple. The process is identical; the only difference is in your mind. So if you *have* attracted some nasty health affliction to yourself, reduce it in your mind to the size of a pimple, let go of all negative thoughts, and then focus on perfect health.

I believe and know that nothing is incurable. At some point in time, every so-called incurable disease has been cured. In my mind, and in the world I create, "incurable" does not exist. . . . It is the world where "miracles" are everyday occurrences. It is a world overflowing with total abundance, where ***all*** *good things exist now, within you. Sounds like heaven, doesn't it? It is.*

Rhonda Byrne

THE SECRET

THE GIFT OF LIFE

Life truly is an amazing gift to be cherished. And if you wise up and learn to generate positive thoughts about yourself and your body and your life as it is now, then it is going to be a life full of good health, well-being, and abundance. And as our old pal Buddha once said, "Health is the greatest gift." So cherish the gift of health - and the gift of life.

REAL STORIES

Sam's Secret

It all started off in my woodworking class. It was in the beginning of summer and class was almost done. I was working on a disk sander to finish up a table I was working on. Well, the wood that I was sanding chipped and flew out of my hands, my left index finger and part of my thumb came into contact with the sander, and my finger got sanded. I still have all of my finger, but it sanded all the way to the bone. When I arrived at the hospital, they told me it couldn't be stitched and that it just had to heal "back to normal."

Well, after a few weeks I couldn't feel much on the finger, and the doctors said I might lose all feeling in the finger permanently. I asked if that would affect my playing the guitar, and he kind of laughed and said, "First off, you are very lucky to be alive – you lost over a pint of blood. However, you will never be able to play guitar again – or even move your finger that well." I was heartbroken, because I am VERY passionate about guitar and singing. But I didn't believe him . . . and so from then on I constantly pictured myself playing guitar again. And then I would try and try, and for a while to no avail.

But I didn't stop there. So that I could move my finger, I soaked it in hot water until my bandage came off. But the scab was fused into the bandage, so I had to slowly tear off my scab. Three times a day, every day, I did this.

And when I had the bandage off, I would move my finger, close my eyes, and picture feeling my whole finger and being able to move it without any trouble of pain again.

I kept doing that every day for two months, and after that I was able to move my finger more, and I could feel all of it without pain. After that I turned to my guitar, and every day I would practice playing and visualizing myself playing without any problems. And after two more months I was playing guitar again and building the muscle back up that was sanded off.

Now, nearly a year later, I can play great, even with the scar.

I have full feeling back in my finger. My doctor said, "I am amazed that you can even feel that finger anymore." I am so grateful that I am able to feel and play again. Music is my life, and thanks to The Secret it's still in my life.

Sam, age 15
Wisconsin, USA

THE SECRET 101

No matter what your current state of health, no matter whether you're unwell or whether you're just really out of shape, consider all the things you are able to do physically, and all the things you enjoy, and then think of all the things you would like to do better. Maybe it's to be healthier, or maybe it's to be fitter or faster or stronger, or maybe it's just to have more stamina - to run, to play, to compete, to dance, to sing, to stay out all night long.

Picture yourself doing just that: running or playing or dancing or singing all night long. Imagine yourself getting right into it - the sights, the sounds, the smells. Feel the feelings from your limbs and muscle fibers to your skin and your outermost nerve endings - feel the tingling sensations. Be that person in your mind, embody that experience. See yourself strong, see yourself powerful, see yourself perfect. And in this state of mind, you can pull out all the tools....

GRATITUDE

For starters, you might like to give thanks for the strength and the fitness and the stamina and the all-around physical well-being to do what you want to do and be what you want to be. Give thanks for living the dream.

VISUALIZATION

Pull out your Photoshop skills, or maybe the scissors and glue, and then cut and paste your own face onto the body of LeBron James or Rihanna or Hugh Jackman or Maria Sharapova. Or whomever you consider to be the ideal physical specimen.

ASK, BELIEVE, RECEIVE

Ask for well-being, fitness, stamina, and strength. Believe that this dream is your birthright and that only your previous limiting thoughts and beliefs can deny you perfect health. And to receive the dream, simply relax and allow the natural flow of well-being. Don't constantly and obsessively weigh yourself, or measure yourself, or check your blood pressure or your cholesterol or your heart rate or your running times, or do anything else that quantifies your success or failure. Just open yourself up to good health and vigor. Believe in your well-being and live as if it is a done deal.

A wise person once said, "If you don't have your health, you don't have anything!" Well, now you know that health is entirely in your hands, in your thoughts, and in your mind. And that means you have power over everything - your body, your well-being, your life - and all because you have ***THE SECRET***...to health.

THE SECRET TO THE WORLD

PLANET EARTH FOREVER

When most people think about the world around them, instead of getting hyper and excited by all the awesome stuff, they direct their energy toward the "bad" stuff: the poverty, the wars, the hunger, the pollution. They see this bad stuff going down, and they feed into it – literally. They study up on some tragic event in great detail and they let it eat away at them. And in that state of depression and anxiety, they take on the grief as a kind of crusade, like it's their personal responsibility to keep such terrible things from happening. And you might be thinking, "Well, isn't it?"

Okay, here's the deal: you can't go taking full responsibility for all the world's tragedies. You just can't put that on yourself. It's fair to say that we all play a part; we all contribute to making the world the way it is. But the bottom line is, you certainly can't *help* the world by stressing out and giving your full attention to all of the bad stuff. Especially if it makes you feel bad. Because by doing that, through the law of attraction, you are actually adding to the problem. It's growing as you give your attention to it!

As an example, you might be worried about the state of the environment. So you focus on all the trees being cut down. You stress about all these trees disappearing and the effect that has on the ecosystem. But your focus and attention on these trees being cut down leads to more trees and entire forests being cut down. It's like your thoughts have turned into a sixty-foot-tall lumberjack belting around the Amazon with a chainsaw!

"What you resist persists."
Carl Jung – psychiatrist

So you can't let yourself get all stressed by the bad stuff in the world because frankly, it's not helping. You have to avoid giving your attention to bad stuff, and you should most definitely think twice about joining in any protest. No matter if it's against global warming or poverty or hunger or terrorism or war or any of that stuff. Because you're just attracting more of that stuff.

Seriously. Think about it.

WAR AND PEACE

Let's take a war protest as an example. Okay, so everyone agrees that war is a total downer, the absolute worst; there's no argument there. But when you protest against war, you're most likely rejecting war and resisting war and hating on war with the intensity and the vibe that protests often generate. Which is why protests so often get to be violent. Even the passive resistance of Mahatma Gandhi and Dr. Martin Luther King Jr. ended in extreme acts of violence. That's because the resistance of violence creates an extremely powerful attraction for more violence. Such intense focus on violence can't help but attract more violence - because what you think about, you bring about.

But there *is* another way. You *can* create an alternative to violence without attracting more violence. And all it requires is the courage to step out from the crowd. Appreciate that strength does not necessarily lie in numbers or in force, but in the power of one applying the most powerful law in the Universe. And when you believe that, you'll see you have more influence to change the world than you ever imagined.

"The world we have created is a product of our thinking; it cannot be changed without changing our thinking."
Albert Einstein – physicist

It's fundamental to the law of attraction: focus on what you want, not on what you don't want. To do that, you may have to resist the urge to join protest rallies with thousands of other angry, disenchanted people. Because as you well know, they're all attracting exactly what they *don't* want.

2-4-6-8, WHO DO WE APPRECIATE?

Instead, you can choose to apply ***THE SECRET***, and you can lead the way, attracting exactly what you *do* want. Focus all your thoughts and power and energy on what you desire; whether that's peace or goodwill or freedom or prosperity for all. Whatever it might be, you're sure to achieve it without any of the resistance or aggression or violence often associated with protest.

Let's cut back to the movie *Hairspray*. At one point Tracy gets herself worked up about racial segregation on TV. She joins in a protest rally, winds up assaulting a cop, and becomes a fugitive from the law. She's suddenly done more harm to the cause than good. Eventually she redeems herself on live TV by uniting black and white in the big dance finale, resolving all racial tensions in the best traditions of the Hollywood happy ending. Notice how a dance celebration succeeds where violent protest failed.

"You must be the change you want to see in the world."
Mahatma Gandhi – spiritual leader

And in life, if you want to see change in the world, you have to imagine that the world already exists exactly the way you want it to be. Picture Earth covered in amazing, pristine forests, breathtaking coastlines, and rolling crystal blue oceans. Or see people the world over partying to celebrate a whole year or maybe a decade of global peace and harmony and goodwill and cooperation and friendship among all of humankind. Or every single man, woman, boy, and girl safe and warm in a comfortable home, with plenty of food and all the money they need, now and forever more. How cool would that be? Imagine dudes like you, happy and content, at peace and living in prosperity. Imagine perfection in all you can see, in all walks of life, all over the world.

POWER UP

Through the power of your vibe and your best intentions, you will attract more thoughts and more people who think just like you. Soon your thoughts and feelings will have helped shape the way everyone thinks, and the law of attraction will ultimately attract this perfect world of peace and happiness and abundance and nature into reality.

And as for the bad stuff that you hear about going on around the world, like war or earthquakes or famine or worse, instead of letting yourself get all depressed and in a funk about it, thereby adding to the problem, what you can do is take the time to send your love and thoughts of well-being, peace, and abundance to all those affected.

You not only create your life with your thoughts, but your thoughts add powerfully to the creation of the world. If you thought that you were insignificant and had no power in this world, think again. Your mind is actually ***shaping*** *the world around you.*

Rhonda Byrne

THE SECRET

Now, that might sound frightening, like a huge responsibility. But just remember that bad things may well happen – things we resist, things we don't want to happen. And we add to those things and make them worse when we focus all of our energy upon them. But we do have the power to change these bad things, to turn them around, by simply focusing on the opposite, focusing on the good, on the things we really want to happen. When we do that, we change the world. How cool is that?

REAL STORIES

Penelope's Secret

I have been consciously living the law of attraction since I first became aware of it when I was nineteen. Living this Universal law has taken me to many places and given me many experiences. I have witnessed the devastating clear-felling of native old-growth forests in Tasmania and Victoria. I became disillusioned with the "anti-logging" campaigns, which brought more of the same because we were focusing on what we did not want and getting more of it.

Recently I became involved in an environmental campaign, however this time with the application of the law of attraction. I created a project that resulted in transforming the attitude of a whole community.

The Save the Mary River Coordinating Group had been campaigning to stop the government from building a dam on the Mary River, in the Sunshine Coast Hinter-

land in Queensland, and were distributing "NO DAM" stickers and signs all around the local area.

Knowing how the law of attraction works, and that people in the Mary Valley would be attracting more DAM by putting out that message, I knew that a new, positive message was needed. Together, we developed a new, inspirational message: "MARY RIVER FOREVER" – a bold statement that claims exactly what we want!

At the Senate Inquiry hearings in Brisbane, there was not a single "NO DAM" sign in sight – it was all "MARY RIVER FOREVER," resulting in great media coverage on all of the main news channels and in the newspapers! People all around the Sunshine Coast have now embraced the concept, and two new stickers have been created – "MARY RIVER FOREVER" and "I LOVE THE MARY" – which are now being distributed on cars everywhere!

The result of this project has been that it has created a surge of positivity in the community, a renewed feeling of hope, and many people have commented on how wonderful the new message is and how happy they are to now support the campaign. This is creating an enormous difference in the attitude people have now. Instead of despairing about the situation, people are feeling more positive and inspired.

My intention is that this concept be applied to environmental and community projects globally. In the face of global warming, pollution, and clearing of precious forests, what is needed is a global shift in consciousness, so that people understand that we can enjoy a wonderful quality of life AND enjoy our natural world. A global shift in awareness would have people worldwide focusing on what kind of world they really want to create for their families and communities, and for future generations.

Penelope
Queensland, Australia

NO NEWS IS GOOD NEWS

If you happen to read the newspapers or watch the evening news, you might be inclined to think of the world as a pretty hostile and frightening place to live. Check it out: every night millions sit glued to the TV as some life-sized Barbie or Ken news anchor spins a line about the latest natural disaster or world conflict or violent crime spree. Scary stuff. Much scarier than anything Stephen King ever imagined.

Truth is, all that bad news is not an accurate reflection of what's really going down. Think about it – six bad things happen in the world in a day, and a million good things happen. What makes the news? The six bad things, of course. And they try to tell you that's where it's at, that's the news. And then people are fearful, and so they attract more real-life horror stories into their own lives, which then feeds the news...and the cycle continues.

So why does the media do it? Why do they spin the hostile Universe angle? Because scary sells. Just ask Stephen King. It's entertainment; it's show business, and the TV news divisions are just responding to what they think their audience wants. And who can blame them? CNN's ratings go through the roof every time something bad happens. So of course every news division all over the world responds by focusing on more bad news. And we keep watching. It's not the news divisions' fault, it's the law of attraction - we attract it.

DROP IN, TURN ON, TUNE OUT

So if you're not into bad news, what can you do about it? Tune out. Simple as that. You don't need to watch it, and there's no law that says you have to. If it doesn't make you feel good, turn it off. Doesn't necessarily make you an obliviot just because you refuse to add to the vibe.

Go find something else to do with that time. And what you'll find is that TV news will respond by delivering something fresh to win you back, maybe even some good news. And that creates a good vibe, creating more good stories, and the world will be exponentially cooler for it.

Remember that what you choose to focus on is always creating what comes into existence. And if what you choose to focus on happens to be a more peaceful, joyous, and friendly Universe, then all the better.

Always remember to make your own call according to what feels right to you. That is, if someone tries to lay a guilt trip on you about war or poverty or some other vital issue, and that guilt trip doesn't make you feel good, don't let them bring you down.

BEWARE THE HYPE

This is especially true with crusading celebrities. Have you ever noticed how the rich and famous have their pet peeves, and they get their heads on TV and so we have to hear all about it? Okay, maybe these issues *are* important, but just stop and think about it. By adding their energy and emotion to the problem, chances are, these celebrities have become part of the problem. Doesn't mean you should be part of the problem too.

The point is, a mouth can say anything - especially a famous one. So it's important not to jump on the bandwagon just because some celeb tells you to. You have to make your own call, so check it out for yourself. After you've had a chance to process what the issue is, and if it's something you feel strongly about, then fair enough, get involved. But don't protest, don't add energy to the problem. Step off and become a part of the solution.

To be fair, some celebs have figured this one out for themselves, and they deserve respect for their selfless deeds and philanthropy. In other words, they're legends for what they do, not what they say. Especially when it's focused on celebrating the good stuff in life. For instance, you might like to give respect to:

- Justin Timberlake, whose foundation advocates music education at a young age
- Mariah Carey, whose holiday camp program aims to inspire and expand the career options of urban teenagers
- Tiger Woods, whose Learning Center seeks to help children through education and personal enrichment
- Oprah Winfrey, who built an entire school for underprivileged South African girls to become the next leaders of their country

These are the true heroes, who use their resources to attract more abundance, more well-being, and more happiness for the world.

HURRY! WHILE STOCKS LAST

And it's crucial that we celebrate abundance, because so many people get all upset about the so-called limitation of the world's resources; that there's not enough stuff to go around. For years we've been told that oil is running out or there's not enough food or water or any of the stuff we need and want. Everyone buys into that notion, and it's what half the wars in the world are all about. It makes people greedy and fearful, hoarding their own stuff, refusing to share, and in some instances, stealing from their neighbors.

And this fear is also why people get so stressed when they think that if everyone on the planet used ***THE SECRET***, we'd all be in catastrophic danger. They figure if everyone can have, do, or be whatever they like, the planet might go into meltdown.

Well, there are a couple of things to consider right there.

NOT EVERYONE'S INTO BLING

First up, everyone's unique. Everyone has different dreams, different interests, different passions. Some may like the more opulent displays of wealth and consumer spending, like cruising around in a fully optioned luxury car, or draping themselves in 24-karat gold, or wearing next season's couture fashions.

But others have more down-to-earth interests. Like back-packing around the world or celebrating nature. Or good food or music or hanging out at the beach.

So there's really no need to stress, because as long as people the world over remain unique and diverse, with different dreams and different desires and different aspirations, there won't ever be lack or limitation. And as long as you know that we can all have or do or be anything, and that we create whatever we want through attraction, you'll be helping to bring an end to all jealousy and greed and hoarding and coveting and fear of going without. Because if you've got all the gear you'll ever need, and if you really do want for nothing, then you won't ever have to give a second thought to what your neighbor's got.

"The ones who are crazy enough to think that they can change the world are the ones who do."

Steve Jobs – co-founder of Apple Inc.

And the other great thing about supply and limitation is that human beings are *übersmart*. No kidding, whenever the world faces a challenge, some clever brainiac uses cutting-edge science and technology and ingenuity to deal with it. Someone develops new farming techniques, or someone invents clean, renewable energy sources. Because when the need and desire is great, we attract the solution and the way.

And that's due in no small part to ***THE SECRET***; when we're a match to what we want, we just have to ASK and BELIEVE. And thanks to the law of attraction, the Universe works through some genius geek somewhere, and lo and behold, we all RECEIVE.

The potential is really there for an unlimited supply of everything you could ever want. Remember that everything in the Universe is energy, and energy cannot be created or destroyed – it simply transforms into other forms of energy. Thus, energy never runs out. It's just waiting to be transformed into the stuff you desire.

And even if everyone in the whole world is in sync with their desires, if everyone wants the exact same thing, the Universe will find a way to transform energy and provide the resources so *everyone* RECEIVES their desire.

> *You are here on this glorious planet, endowed with this wonderful power, to create your life! There are no limits to what you can create for You, because your ability to think is unlimited! . . . The Universe offers* ***all*** *things to* ***all*** *people through the law of attraction. You have the ability to choose what you want to experience. Do you want there to be enough for you and for everyone? Then choose that and know, "There is abundance of all things." "There is an unlimited supply." "There is so much magnificence." Each of us has the ability to tap into that unlimited invisible supply through our thoughts and feelings, and bring it into our experience. So choose for You, because you're the only one who can.*

Rhonda Byrne

THE SECRET

REAL STORIES

Yoshimitsu's Secret

Man, the beautiful creation of endless possibilities as a result of the one mind, crafted through the quadromillions of molecular possibilities and Universal shifting. Never have I realized that so well until now. The Universe's repetition of the law that's most important – what keeps us together – is the most noticeable of its kind. As magnets attract, as gravity holds planets, and as a kiss to your love brings you closer, our Universe christens us within its warm arms.

Sometimes I look at the many things around me and cry with happiness, and sometimes I leave offerings to the Earth, and thank the Great Mother for such a wonderful gift she allows us to have. As we reside in her womb, I've always wondered, after we've outgrown this world, what beautiful thing shall we receive next?

Yoshimitsu, age 13
Virginia, USA

The Universe is awesome, no doubt about it, and your thoughts and your vibe are a major part of its creation.

Picture this: the Universe is like some vast concrete wall, and all the best graffiti artists have come together to collaborate on a massive mural of Earth, each artist inking their tags and stencils and 'pieces according to their own flow, but each one adding to the vision of Earth, adding to its creation. And you've just been tossed a spray can. What are you going to paint? Some mediocre scrawl or throw up? Some act of vandalism that detracts from the vision of the other artists? Or are you going to step up and create your own masterpiece, your inspirational vision of Planet Earth?

It's all on you.

Well, this is for real; forget the spray can, forget the graffiti mural. Your thoughts and feelings add to the magnificence and beauty or to the destruction and vandalism of the planet, the same way you would add to a concrete mural. If you are bold and imaginative with your thoughts and feelings, you'll bring beauty and magnificence. But if you are careless and cynical in what you think and how you feel, you may as well block the entire mural of Earth, capping the creativity of all those who have gone before you.

Now, you probably thought you were small and powerless on this vast and great planet. You are not powerless; in fact, you have all the power! Like any artist, you create perfection in your life and on planet Earth with your thoughts and feelings. Simply feel the good and you'll create the good. Feel love, feel gratitude, and have faith that everything on planet Earth can be, and actually is, perfect just as you imagined it.

"Think of all the beauty still left around you and be happy."
Anne Frank – author

THE SECRET 101

Consider the awesome beauty of the world around you. Now consider your absolute favorite places in the world - all the cool sites, all the best locations. Or maybe just somewhere you love to hang out.

People may try to tell you that your favorite place won't last, that someone sometime is going to wreck it forever. After all, that's progress. But you have to know by now that those rules don't apply to you. Because you have the power to attract whatever you want.

So if visiting this cool place (or maybe even living there) is part of your dream, what you should do is photograph or download an image of it and stick it on your wall or mirror. If you've got some skills in graphics or drawing, do one better - Photoshop yourself *in* the picture.

Once it's complete, print out a copy and stick it up where you'll always see it. Maybe make it your screen saver. Upload it to your Facebook page if you have one.

And look at it as often as you can. Breathe in deeply and feel the gratitude and appreciation in your heart for this amazing place. Feel the feelings of being there - the smells, the sights, the sounds, the sensations. Know that it will be there as long as you wish.

And believe and know that your favorite place - and, in fact, the whole wide, beautiful world as you see it - will be there for you for the rest of your life. Because you hold the power. And that's ***THE SECRET***...to the world.

THE SECRET TO YOU

FROM ZERO TO HERO

Whether or not you are into science, you'll be interested to learn that ***THE SECRET*** is in total harmony with the latest findings in quantum physics. So if that's your thing, or if you're at least open to the notion, then you can use these scientific discoveries to your benefit. Check this out....

Everything in the Universe is made of energy. Animal, mineral, vegetable...even a glass of water; they're all made of the same stuff: energy. What makes them different is that they're vibrating at different speeds. Even when two things are almost identical, the subtle differences are measured in vibrations.

Think of the glass of water. At low vibration the water becomes ice. And at high vibration water becomes steam. So water can easily become ice or steam, simply by changing vibration. It doesn't necessarily go anywhere, it just changes vibration. Even as a vapor, you might not be able to see it due to the vibrations being so high, but it still exists; the "water" is still there. So if anyone ever tries to tell you there's a water shortage, that we've run out of water, you'll know better.

And that's because water is, in essence, energy. It doesn't disappear or evaporate into nothing or get used up in the shower; it simply slows down or speeds up to become something else. You see, water – or energy – at the subatomic, microscopic, infinitesimal level, can never be created or destroyed. It always existed and it always will exist.

Now stay with it, because this is pretty trippy....

It's the same deal with you. Just like water, you always existed and you always will. The true essence of you, the spirit of you, the pure energy of you, those subatomic particles of energy that you are composed of, have existed for billions of years, and always will. How cool is that?! You are actually billions of years old! And you thought your grandpa was crusty old!

FOREVER AND EVER

Seriously, scientists and quantum physicists will confirm this idea that energy can never be created or destroyed, it simply changes form. And because you are made of energy, therefore you cannot ever be destroyed. You are eternal, you are infinite, and for you, there is life beyond the physical. Now, that doesn't mean you have to go all Jennifer Love Hewitt and start whispering with dead people. It just means that the energy of you will last forever. And not only that, but the energy that's you is just part of one humongous field of energy that makes up everything.

That means you and your best friend and even your worst enemy are all part of the same energy field. You are all connected. And the freaky thing about that is it's not just your physical being, your body, that's part of this sea of energy. It's also your thoughts, your feelings, your imagination, and your entire vibe. That's all energy too, and it connects you into this energy field and intermingles with everyone else all across the planet. It's like there's this One Universal Mind and we're all a part of it. We are all One.

Some call this the "collective unconscious," a term first coined by eminent psychiatrist and father of analytical psychology, Carl Jung. Or some call it "One Love," as that Bob Marley song goes.

Or you might think of it as the Matrix, except you don't have to stress about Keanu Reeves saving you from life as a human Duracell. Indeed, this is like a friendly Matrix, connecting every human being, animal, plant, and mineral on Earth. And you connect to everything by simply focusing on that human being, that animal, that plant, or that mineral with your mind. We are all One. Pretty cool, huh?

But so what? What does this mean? Well, for starters, it means you are never alone; you are always connected, because we are One.

But on the flip side, it means that if you're messing with people, then that mess will only return to harm *you*. Since you're connected with everyone via this One Universal

Mind (otherwise known as The Matrix), bad vibes toward someone else means bad vibes to you too.

YOUR OWN WORST ENEMY

It's the same deal with competition. When you compete against others, you're often beating up on yourself. And you can never win like this, even if it seems like you have at the time.

Sure, sports can be fun - even a good earner if you're talented enough. But it's important that you don't let competition take over your life. People who take on a competitive mind-set often find themselves competing in business, in relationships, in love, and in life itself. And thanks to the law of attraction, as you compete in order to be "the best," you'll attract fierce competition - and eventually you'll be the loser. It's as inevitable in ordinary life as it is in the sports arena, whether that be one-on-one hoops in the schoolyard or even the NBA. If you search hard enough and long enough, there's only one certainty, and that is: you're going to find someone to beat you. Even Michael Jordan got beat occasionally.

"Just play. Have fun. Enjoy the game."
Michael Jordan – basketball champion

See, life is not a race to the finish line. It's not like we're all on this desperate sprint to take a running dive headfirst into a grave. Life is about the journey of living, and having a great time while you're at it. Kick back and enjoy the ride. Get competition out of your mind, and instead live creatively. Focus on *your* dreams and *your* visions, and don't look sideways at what other people are doing. Be the very best that *you* can be - whatever you're doing.

That's what winning really is... not crushing some opponent who's not so good, but being all *you* can be. There's no victory in finding someone inferior to compare yourself with. And likewise, there's no point getting mad because someone is better than you at something. Just take pride in your own efforts, and enjoy discovering the extent of your abilities.

HEROES

Steven Bradbury

Leading into the 2002 Winter Olympics, speed skater Steven Bradbury was edging toward the end of his career. Having spent twelve years on the circuit, Bradbury had raced and fought with the best and had the battle scars to prove it: two broken vertebrae, spinal traction, 111 stitches where a blade had pierced his thigh, and losing 80 percent of his blood onto the ice. Now the elder statesman of the field, Bradbury was just hoping to do his best - even if that meant coming in last. Yet he had the great good fortune to qualify for the 1000-meter short track final thanks largely to disqualifications and collisions through the heats and semifinals.

And so he lined up alongside four much stronger, faster, and younger skaters, each of them fully prepared to win at all costs. Bradbury decided not to feed into that, but to hang back in the hope that their aggression might result in another collision. And who knew, maybe he'd sneak a bronze medal. . . .

Throughout the race he tried to stick with the pack, but they were way too fast. Yet no-one could have predicted the carnage of the very last corner. All four adrenaline-fueled competitors brought one another crashing down on the ice, bloody and bruised, as back-marker and last-man-standing Bradbury skated by to claim the most unlikely gold.

Some say Steven Bradbury is the luckiest gold medal winner in Olympic history. Truth is, he'd spent twelve years competing like a maniac, yet in that competitive mindset, he'd never reached his full potential. For the first time, he skated just to be the best that he could be. And that's what makes him a true champion. You see, it's not all about winning gold.

"You are never really playing an opponent. You are playing yourself, your own highest standards, and when you reach your limits, that is real joy."
Arthur Ashe – tennis champion

Whenever you find yourself competing for something, just remember that we're all connected, that we all have a link to the One Universal Mind, that we are all a part of the Matrix, that we are all One. So if you compete, you're really competing with yourself.

And remember, too, that the Matrix connects every human being, animal, plant, and mineral on Earth at the level of energy. So that includes thoughts, feelings, imagination, everything. Going back to the dawn of time, it's all stored on this giant database belonging to the Matrix, and we all add to this Matrix with every thought. Einstein tells us that time is an illusion, that the past, present, and future are all part of the Universal database.

So that means it's completely pointless racing to be first, because every thought, every dream, and every *possibility* is already available. They already exist because everything is stored in the One Universal Mind - otherwise known as the Matrix. And it's just waiting for *you* to tap in.

This is really sweet because every creation in history - every fine idea, every brilliant invention that you use every day - like the iPhone or the Wii, or even classics like Ray-Ban aviators and those Reeboks with the straps - were all sourced from the One Universal Mind, whether the creators realized it or not.

And you can plug into this too. The same way Keanu and Co. tapped into the Matrix to download the knowledge of how to fly a helicopter just when they needed it, so too can you receive the inspiration, the motivation, and the know-how to have, do, or be whatever you choose. Simply use your imagination and *ASK, BELIEVE, RECEIVE.*

"Whether you think you can or think you can't, either way you are right."

Henry Ford – founder of Ford Motor Company

Do you think you can do this? Do you think you can tap the Matrix and do anything you choose? YES, YOU CAN! The only reason you can't is because you say you can't and you convince yourself you can't. Truth is, you *can* achieve and do anything you want with this knowledge.

In the past you've probably underestimated how brilliant you are. Well, now you're wise to the fact that you are part of this One Universal Mind, this collective unconscious, this Matrix, and that you can draw anything you want from it. Pretty awesome!

WOULDN'T IT BE GREAT IF SOMEONE INVENTED...

The Matrix is quite probably giving you clues to your potential brilliance right now. For instance, have you ever had the thought, "Wouldn't it be great if someone invented ________" [*fill in the blank*]? Well, who's to say that you can't be that person who invents that ________ [*fill in the blank*]?

And the best part is, having asked the question "Wouldn't it be great...?" you're now attracting all sorts of thoughts and theories and creative ideas and technical solutions shared by anyone who ever had the same brainwave at any point in human history. Your thoughts attract their ideas. How cool is that? It's like you don't even need to be a genius or anything to suddenly have these genius thoughts pop into your head. Just open your eyes and your ears, observe what's missing or needed in that "Wouldn't it be great...?" kind of fashion, think that first thought, and *BAM!*...you're halfway there.

WHO WANTS TO BE A BAJILLIONAIRE?

Check out the inventors of YouTube. YouTube started with three young guys who just wanted to share videos taken at a party, but the files were too big to email. "Why doesn't someone invent a website to upload and share video clips?" they asked themselves. And so they pooled their resources and did exactly that, building a $1.65 billion company inside eighteen months.

Likewise, the nineteen-year-old Harvard student behind Facebook wondered why no-one had ever created an online version of those student photo books they hand out at college. So with a little help from his friends, he stepped up and created this social networking website for schools, and suddenly it became a worldwide phenomenon. And just like the YouTube dudes, he's now a dot-com gazillionaire.

Interesting that in both cases, they were not the first to come up with what they created - video file sharing or social networking websites. They just checked out what was missing, what the world needed, and then tapped the Matrix for ideas. They then followed up with all the best theories and methods and processes, and found the best possible solutions. So it wasn't about competing, or about being first. It was about attracting inspiration from the One Universal Mind. And the genius solutions just rolled right in.

SHADOWS OF DOUBT

Still, a lot of people have doubts about their creative potential and their ability to tap the Matrix. They talk themselves down and convince themselves that this is all for someone else, not them. They'll say things like:

- "Maybe you can do it, but I can't."
- "I'm not smart enough."
- "I'm not into that sort of thing."
- "You don't understand what I'm dealing with."
- "I've got issues – you don't."

Well, here's the lowdown: everybody's got issues. Everybody has to deal with something. If you think your life sucks, check this out:

- Halle Berry was homeless and had to sleep in a New York City shelter when she was a struggling actor.
- Rob Thomas from Matchbox Twenty was homeless for three years, living on the beach and sleeping on park benches.

- Joss Stone has dyslexia and dropped out of school at age sixteen.
- Christina Aguilera and her mother were victims of physical abuse at the hands of her father.
- Oprah Winfrey was molested and physically abused by relatives at age nine, ran away from home, and became pregnant by the time she was fourteen.

No matter how bad things seem, there's bound to be someone worse off than you. And more than likely, that someone has made a huge success of his or her life despite having a worse handicap than the one you're currently dealing with.

"No matter how hard the past, one can always begin again today."
Buddha – spiritual teacher

Understand that you are not condemned to being stuck in your past. As these famous names prove, you are not just your past. Sure, that's part of you, and maybe it even helps define you and inspire you. But it's entirely up to you whether your past acts as an anchor or a launch pad. Make the choice: you can choose to play the victim and stay the victim, or change the script, stick the S on your chest, and become a hero.

In the movie *Sky High* all the teenage superheroes of tomorrow are classified on their first day as either heroes or sidekicks, according to the faculty's assessment of their potential. And life's like that - someone's always wanting to classify you and pigeonhole you and tell you what you can and can't do. In *Sky High* the fate of the world is in the balance, and it all comes down to the sidekicks playing above their potential and becoming heroes in their own right. Likewise for you, don't let anyone limit you or cast you as a sidekick or a victim or a damsel in distress.

WHEN YOU PLAY THE VICTIM, YOU STAY THE VICTIM

Wouldn't you rather be the hero? Of course you would. So make a choice. Don't play the victim and don't stay the victim. Don't be a hostage to your past circumstances or events.

And the first step is to let go of the past. Don't hold grudges. Why give up some of your valuable energy and brain space to some random from your past whom you don't even care for? Remember, your thoughts are powerful, so don't waste them on people who no longer matter. Forgive and forget, and get on with feeling good and focusing on the stuff you're really into.

REAL STORIES

KC's Secret

It was a sunny and quiet afternoon in the sleepy remote town. Everybody was at home after a busy morning on the farm. Suddenly, a woman burst into the street with bare feet and yelled, "Fire! Fire! My house has caught on fire! Fire! Fire!" It was my mother!

Soon everybody in the town gathered around. Some ran to help put out the fire by passing a bucket from man to man and using the garden hose. We children had already escaped, and watched this horrendous scene from the far end of the street. We were petrified, scared, and stunned, and my heart was pounding so hard that I thought it was going to leap out of my chest. I knew who was responsible....

Finally, the fire was put out when the fire rescue team arrived. Everyone was glad the fire didn't spread to the other houses, but my family's wooden home was destroyed, and nothing was left.

For many people, it was the end of the disaster. But at the bottom of my heart, I knew this was just the beginning of a chapter for an eight-year-old country boy. It was me who accidentally started the fire by playing with candles in one of the bedrooms. I told Mother about it when I realized the curtain caught on fire, but it was too late. The flames quickly spread throughout the room.

"Fire! Fire!" That scream is still in my head. The fire produced a "superstar" in a negative way. The kids at school criticized me, as did close relatives. They saw me as an evil child. Some even barred me from visiting them. Of course, the harshest blame came from my father. I remember how he abused me, how mother ignored me, and relatives were nasty to me. My position in the home was changed from a beloved kid to one hated by everyone.

I didn't intentionally set the fire. I wasn't an arsonist! If setting the fire was considered a crime, haven't I already paid the price over the last seven years for my wrongdoing?

Even though I did manage to emerge from the "bottom of the sea" and see the light, my life has had many setbacks and unfortunate consequences from those early years. People always say, "If you believe in yourself, anything is possible." But in my case, I always had doubts about myself. My lack of confidence enforced my feelings of never having any good luck. In other words, I simply didn't believe good things would happen to me.

Ultimately, it was The Secret that opened my heart. For all these years my anger and lack of forgiveness toward these people haunted me. But did my anger hurt them? No. The Secret is right – if you have anger and hatred and such negative thoughts about people, it will return to harm no-one else but you. And if you do not let your past go, you literally bring more obstacles into your life.

According to The Secret, the way to do it is to forgive. I want to forgive my father and anyone who has intentionally or unintentionally hurt me. I've begun to think some good things about these people. My results – I would never come to this world without my parents, and I wouldn't have any chance to be surrounded by all the amazing people I know today. It was my mother who worked day and night for every penny in order to bring up her six children after my father passed away. I love you, Mom!

Inevitably, The Secret has greatly influenced my life. Through this book, it made me realize how powerful our thoughts are, and how we can change things by changing our thoughts. The Secret has given me a guideline in finding the crucial key to open the real secrets which lie in my heart, that will allow an abundance of prosperities to flow in.

KC
Florida, USA

THE SECRET 101

Sometimes, if you want to let go of your past and get on with feeling good, you need to switch things up with a personal makeover. But unlike the TV makeover shows, we're not talking cosmetics, a new 'do, a tighter bod, or even new clothes. This is all about your vibe and how to make over the way you feel inside. And as with all makeovers, it's out with the old and in with the new.

The first thing you need to trash are all those self-defeating perceptions that start with "I can't" or "I'm not" or "I'll never." Like "I can't do that" or "I'm not strong enough for that" or "I'll never be rich enough to afford that." You need to ditch those thoughts and replace them with the exact opposite.

That's where ***affirmations*** come in. Affirmations are like these mission statements that you say to yourself over and over again until they sink in and become habit. They're affirmative statements in present tense, making out like the mission is already a reality.

"I am the greatest. I said that even before I knew I was."
Muhammad Ali – boxing champion

Right there is a massive tip. The first two words, "I am," are the most powerful words you'll ever use. Because whatever comes after that is what you create. So if you want to get all medieval on your self-defeating thoughts and counter all that bad stuff, you should decide what you really want and then stick "I am" on the front. Here are some more examples you might want to use:

- I am unique and valuable.
- I am beautiful inside and out.
- I am full of great ideas.

- I am extremely creative.
- I am able to do anything I set my mind to.
- I am healthy and strong and perfect just the way I am.
- I am self-confident and I always know the right thing to say and do.

You can try writing seven affirmations each day, right after doing your lists of present and future gratitudes. Whether you repeat the same affirmations each day or come up with new ones, just make sure you genuinely feel them each time, and make sure they fire you up and resonate with your vibe. And read them aloud, ideally while looking in a mirror. Make them your personal challenge to yourself, your code of behavior, a standard you have to live up to each and every day.

Once you've got your affirmations all set, it's time to turbo-charge them. You see, affirmations are cool, but if you really want to give them some grunt, try visualizing at the same time. Picture yourself being unique or brilliant or beautiful or strong. Feel what it would feel like to really achieve your vision - to live and walk and ***be*** your affirmation. And then you're really on the path to creating the perfect ***YOU***.

HOW PERFECT

Okay, you want to hear something wack?

Check this out: Jesus, Buddha, Confucius, Mohammad - in fact, the enlightened messiahs from every religion all readily agree - ***YOU*** are already perfect. ***YOU*** are divine.

You're like a god in human form. You're a genius. You've got access to the Matrix. And you can create anything you choose.

> *You are all power. You are all wisdom. You are all intelligence. You are perfection. You are magnificence. You are the creator, and you are creating the creation of You on this planet.*
>
> Rhonda Byrne
> **THE SECRET**

It's true, you have the most powerful ability to create. In fact, you are creating art right this very moment. You are creating a magnificent story. You are creating life...your own ***SECRET*** life.

THE SECRET TO LIFE

WELCOME TO THE GOOD LIFE

If you want to live the life of your dreams, if you want every day to seem like an adventure, if you want love and happiness on tap now and for the rest of your days, then it makes a lot of sense to figure out why you're on this planet, right here, right now. To know what the plan is, what your purpose is in life.

Maybe you've thought about these pretty humongous concepts at one time or another, or maybe you haven't. But one thing's for sure, if you've been waiting for some guru to break it all down for you, then you're going to be left hanging for a long time.

The thing is, you're not in Kansas anymore, Dorothy, and guess what? There's no yellow brick road, and certainly no fake wizard hiding behind a curtain who can clue you in. So you're going to have to figure this out for yourself.

But you see, it's really so simple, this great mystery that's stumped people for thousands of years. ***THE SECRET*** to life is this:

YOU ARE HERE TO ENJOY YOURSELF

That's it! No big complicated deal. Your major obligation is to have a good time.

"Life is meant to be fun, and joyous, and fulfilling."
Jim Henson – creator of the Muppets

Put another way:

"I believe that the very purpose of our life is to seek happiness."
The Dalai Lama – spiritual leader

Now, what more convincing do you need? The spiritual leader of Tibetan Buddhism and the voice of Kermit the Frog agree: the whole point of life is to have fun, to seek happiness, to be happy. That is your one and only purpose in life.

Often times people confuse their purpose in life with their job, their family business, their pre-planned career path, their education, or the expectations of others. And that leads to unhappiness, which is clearly the total opposite of your purpose in life.

Now, if the Dalai Lama and Jim Henson have the truth down, and your purpose in life really is just to have fun and be happy, then you have a responsibility to have fun, be happy, and to shine your light of enthusiasm upon the world. Your journey, your direction in life, your reason for getting yourself out of bed every morning, should be whatever *YOU* decide, whatever *YOU* choose. So why not choose things that make you feel good, that excite you, that make you happy?

As you feel good, as you experience happiness, you will attract more experiences and feelings of happiness. And through these experiences that you've attracted, it will become bleedingly obvious what it is that you most love to do.

You will very soon find that one thing that has you tingling with anticipation. The one thing that gets your heart pumping, your lungs bursting, and your mind racing. Find *that* and you'll have a life filled with purpose and passion.

"All you have to do in life is be passionate and enthusiastic and you will have a wonderful life."
Steve Irwin – the Crocodile Hunter

Remember where this journey started, when you wrote a list of your favorite things – all the stuff you're into? And then you cut it back to three to establish your purpose, your passion, your motivation in life?

Revisit that and try the same thing again now that you know you can have, do, or be anything you want.

. . . . . .

Has anything changed? Are you clearer now in knowing what it is you want to do with your life? In knowing your passion?

The amazing thing is that as you discover your passion and commit yourself to it, everything else will fall into place, and your path will light up before your very eyes. The law of attraction will bring a bunch of cool things, people, circumstances, and opportunities into your life, all because you are dialed in and giving off the vibe.

And what you'll also find is that your passion is key to your vibe and your happiness. For instance, if ever you find yourself frustrated, angry, or unhappy, it's a sure bet that you're not doing the thing you've identified as your passion. In fact, your frustration is probably a sign that you are being kept from your passion. So your goal is to clear those blocks to get yourself back on track and in sync with your passion. And then happiness will follow.

"Passion makes the world go round."
Ice-T – hip-hop singer, actor

Knowing your passion can also help you if you're getting pressure from other people to follow a certain path in your life – to apply to a certain school, study a particular subject, go into a certain profession, join a club or social group, take up a sport or musical instrument or lifestyle or religion – even if it's just not your thing.

TEEN CHOICE

A lot of the time these choices that other people try to push on you, while they're well intentioned, probably don't get you particularly excited or passionate. That's a clue; it's telling you something. Sure, listen to people's ideas and opinions, but in the end make up your own mind, and choose what excites ***YOU***.

Because here's the drill... nobody ever excelled at something they didn't enjoy. Just ask Oscar-winner Reese Witherspoon. Reese's folks were both medical professionals, so it was just assumed she would go into medicine. But her passion is acting. That's why she excels in front of a camera, and why she almost certainly would NOT have made a good doctor. Not because she's not smart enough, rather because of her passion. In her Academy Awards acceptance speech, Reese summed up her philosophy: *"You know, I'm just trying to matter, and live a good life, and make work that means something to somebody."*

Seems like a fair ambition for anyone.

THE POWER OF ONE

When you first picked up this book and started this journey, maybe you didn't exactly know what you wanted to do with your life.... Maybe because you've had your dreams beaten out of you. Maybe you stopped believing in hope and dreams and miracles. Maybe you stopped believing in ***YOU***.

But now that you know ***THE SECRET***, you can achieve things you might have thought were impossible, or things you thought were for *other* people to achieve. You have the power and the ability to have whatever, do whatever, and be whatever you choose. It's all on you.

What you do with this power is entirely up to you. It's in your hands. Whether you decide to use it, or whether you decide not to use it, it's totally your call and it's all okay either way. Whatever you choose is right for ***YOU***.

"When you realize how perfect everything is, you will tilt your head back and laugh at the sky."
Buddha – *spiritual teacher*

This moment in the history of the world – right here, right now – is the most awesome time ever. Check it out: you're going to see the impossible become possible, in every field of human endeavor, including sports, health, entertainment, art, technology, and science. Surrender all your thoughts of limitation and doubt, and you'll totally experience the unlimited potential of humankind. And, of course, ***YOU***.

The Secret is within you. And the more you use the power within you, the more you will draw it to you. You will reach a point where you won't need to practice anymore, because you will Be the power, you will Be the perfection, you will Be the wisdom, you will Be the intelligence, you will Be the love, you will Be the joy. . . .

The earth turns on its orbit for You. The oceans ebb and flow for You. The birds sing for You. The sun rises and it sets for You. The stars come out for You. Every beautiful thing you see, every wondrous thing you experience, is all there, for You. Take a look around. None of it can exist, without You. No matter who you thought you were, now you know the Truth of Who You Really Are. You are the master of the Universe. You are the heir to the kingdom. You are the perfection of Life. And now you know The Secret.

Rhonda Byrne

THE SECRET

So now that you know ***THE SECRET***, and you've started to live ***THE SECRET***, you ought to appreciate just how significant and special you really are. Accept that you are the future and that you will lead the way. And know that in years to come, people will look back and say, "This was the generation that figured it all out and gained a new understanding. This was the generation that found the answers."

The world will be a better place because you dared to dream. And better still, you've started to live those dreams for ***YOU***.

The power of ***THE SECRET*** lives on in ***YOU***.